Sophocles'
Oedipus the King

CONTINUUM READER'S GUIDES

Continuum Reader's Guides are clear, concise and accessible introductions to key texts in literature and philosophy. Each book explores the themes, context, criticism and influence of key works, providing a practical introduction to close reading, guiding students towards a thorough understanding of the text. They provide an essential, up-to-date resource, ideal for undergraduate students.

Reader's Guides available from Continuum:

Ovid's 'Metamorphoses', Genevieve Liveley

A READER'S GUIDE

Sophocles' *Oedipus the King*

SEÁN SHEEHAN

continuum

Continuum International Publishing Group

The Tower Building   80 Maiden Lane
11 York Road   Suite 704
London SE1 7NX   New York NY 10038

www.continuumbooks.com

British Library Cataloguing-in-Publication Data
A catalogue record for this book is available from the British Library.

ISBN: HB: 978-1-4411-0799-2
PB: 978-1-4411-9824-2

Library of Congress Cataloging-in-Publication Data
Sheehan, Seán, 1951-
Sophocles' "Oedipus the King" : a reader's guide / Seán Sheehan.
    p. cm. – (Reader's guides)
Includes bibliographical references and index.
ISBN 978-1-4411-0799-2 (hardcover) – ISBN 978-1-4411-9824-2 (pbk.)
1. Sophocles. Oedipus Rex. 2. Oedipus (Greek mythology) in literature.
I. Title. II. Title: Oedipus the King: a reader's guide. III. Series.

PA4413.O7S54 2011
882'.01–dc23

2011027655

Typeset by Newgen Imaging Systems Pvt Ltd, Chennai, India
Printed and bound in India

CONTENTS

CHAPTER ONE

Contexts

Sophocles

Oedipus the King, known also as *Oedipus Rex* (from the Latin *'rex'* for king) and as *Oedipus Tyrannus* (from the Greek *'turannos'* for ruler), is the best known of the ancient Greek dramas. Aristotle, writing nearly a century after the play's first production, refers to it as just *Oidipous* (the Latinized form of which is *Oedipus*), and the *Tyrannus* that came into the title may have arisen from a need to distinguish it from Sophocles' later play, *Oedipus at Colonus,* that deals with Oedipus at the end of his life, after the events recorded in the earlier drama. *Tyrannus,* a version of the Greek *turannos* which gives us the word tyrant, was used as a neutral term for a sole ruler who did not acquire power through hereditary descent from a king. Oedipus as the political ruler of Thebes through his marriage to the widow of the previous king is known as *turannos* in *Oedipus* without the pejorative sense we give to the word tyrant (although it could carry such overtones in Sophocles' age).

Oedipus, one of the seven plays by Sophocles that have survived complete, is dated by scholars to around 429–425,[1] though there is no conclusive evidence for this. More definite is the date of 402/1 for *Oedipus at Colonus,* produced posthumously by his grandson who was also named Sophocles.

Sophocles' birthplace, just outside of Athens, was part of the region known as Attica, divided from the neighbouring region of Boeotia by the Cithaeron mountain range. Thebes, the largest city in Boeotia, was a traditional enemy of Athens. Sophocles, born between 497 and 494, was around five years old when an invading Persian force was defeated by an Athenian army. Ten years later the Persians invaded for a second time and were again defeated, this time by an alliance of Greek city states. The city of Thebes, supporting the Persians, was not part of this alliance. One of the stories that have come down from ancient sources, the reliability of which cannot be taken on trust, is that Sophocles led a chorus of boys, playing his lyre, at the celebrations that followed in the city of Athens after the defeat of the Persians.

Sophocles died in 406/5, just two years before the defeat of Athens in the Peloponnesian War, a long-running conflict with Sparta and her allies which included Thebes. *Oedipus* is set in Thebes and was probably first performed in the early years of the Peloponnesian War. When Athens was defeated in this war, Thebes called for the complete destruction of the city, an act which would have involved mass executions and the enslavement of its female population (a wartime act carried out by Athens on the population of Melos during Sophocles' lifetime).

Sophocles was a very successful playwright, writing at least 120 plays (of which seven have survived in their entirety and at least eighteen in fragments, including some lines from his lost *Progeny* that were discovered in 2005) and winning the first prize nearly twenty times at the drama competitions for the City Dionysia festival. He was in his late twenties when he won his first prize in 468, over sixty at the time of *Oedipus*. It is known that he held the public office of Treasurer in 443/2 and shortly afterwards, perhaps the following year, was elected general (*strategós*, the highest public post in Athens) for a military campaign undertaken by Athens in the Peloponnesian War. In 413, during the course of this war and after the failure of the Athenian expedition to Sicily, Sophocles had been a magistrate at Athens.

The Oedipus myths

The stories that are dramatized in Greek tragedy come from tales that were passed down orally across generations, nearly always involving heroes that point back to a period in Greek history known as the Mycenean age (1600–1200). They are the basis of the tales recorded in Homer's epics (written three centuries before Sophocles) and in the works of Hesiod and Pindar and many of them found visual representation in works of sculpture on temples and paintings on vases. As well as featuring famous heroes these stories often involve gods and goddesses who at different levels interact with the heroic but still mortal individuals and the resultant whole is a body of myths that gave the Greeks a means of not just representing their cultural beliefs, but a way of probing and questioning these beliefs. 'Myth', as William Golding put it, ' is a feeling towards something which we know to be significant and cannot tell why'.[2] Perhaps this helps to understand why there are Oedipus *myths*, not a single tale with an unalterable form but a set of variations on a theme that features a man killing his father and marrying his mother.

In book eleven of *The Odyssey* Odysseus recounts his visit to Hades and whom he saw there, which includes Jocasta (Epikaste) the mother and wife of Oedipus (Oidipodes):

I saw the beautiful Epikaste, Oidipodes' mother,
who in ignorance of her mind had done a monstrous
thing when she married her own son. He killed his father
and married her, but the gods soon made it all known to mortals.
But he, for all his sorrows in beloved Thebes continued
to be lord over the Kadmeians, all through the bitter designing
of the gods; while she went down to Hades of the gates, the strong one,
knotting a noose and hanging sheer from the high ceiling,
in the constraint of her sorrow, but left to him who survived her
all the sorrows that are brought to pass by a mother's furies.[3]

In this account, the discovery of what happened was brought about by the gods, not detective work on the part of Oedipus, and as in a line from the *Iliad* (referring to someone who 'came once to Thebes and the tomb of Oidipous after his downfall'[4]) the indication is that Oedipus remained in Thebes. And if the marriage of Jocasta and Oedipus was short-lived ('the gods soon made it all known to mortals'), then presumably his children were the result of a second marriage. In the *Thebais*, part of an epic cycle of poems dealing with the history of Thebes, written some time after Homer and of which only fragments survive, Oedipus also remains in Thebes after the death of his wife.

What these poems indicate is that for the ancient Greeks there was no authoritative version of the Oedipus myth, variations could occur and the emphasis shift, and an audience watching Sophocles' drama would not have known exactly how the play was going to begin, proceed or end. According to Pausanias, writing in the second century CE, a part of an epic cycle known as the *Oidipodeia* has Oedipus remarrying and in one account his second wife is a sister of Jocasta. This last detail (and in the light of the quotation from Homer above that suggests Jocasta committed suicide soon after her marriage) allows for the possibility that it cannot even be taken for granted that Jocasta is Oedipus' wife at the start of Sophocles' drama. The myths surrounding Oedipus would, it seems, allow for Oedipus marrying Jocasta and having children by her, but that she subsequently dies, perhaps by suicide but without revealing to her husband her motive, and Oedipus then remarrying, this time to her sister. It could be that Sophocles makes theatrical mileage out of this possibility for the first six hundred lines of *Oedipus* so that, for example, in the scene where Teiresias tells Oedipus that he is the killer of Laius and lives 'in foulest shame unconsciously' (366–367), this would still make sense if Jocasta was no longer alive. From this point of view, and it has been argued for,[5] Jocasta is only revealed to be alive and well when she makes her dramatic entrance during the argument between Oedipus and Creon and is identified by the chorus ('I see Jocasta coming from the house', 632). Such an argument may seem far-fetched, but only perhaps because our knowledge of details of the Oedipus story is so likely to derive from acquaintance with Sophocles' version that we assume his telling of the story was always the one already known by audiences. The knowledge that this was not the case introduces a level of uncertainty for an Athenian audience watching Sophocles' play that is not always taken into account.

Aeschylus wrote a trilogy based on the Oedipus myth that won the first prize at the City Dionysia in 467 and although the first and second of these plays, called *Laius* and *Oedipus* respectively, have been lost (as has the accompanying satyr play called *Sphinx*) the third one, *Seven Against Thebes*, survives and it tells the story of how two sons of Oedipus, Eteocles and Polynices, kill each other in a dispute over the Theban throne. And nearly twenty years after Sophocles' *Oedipus*, Euripides could write a drama, *The Phoenician Women*, in which Jocasta does not commit suicide after discovering who she has married and remains alive after

Oedipus has blinded himself.[6] And in an early copy of this play a scholiast quotes two lines from a play that Euripides wrote about Oedipus, but which has now been lost. In this lost play, Oedipus' blindness is not self-inflicted but carried out by others and seemingly against his will, as indicated by the scholiast's comment:

> In [Euripides'] *Oedipus*, however, Laius' attendants blinded him: 'But we threw the son of Polybus to the ground and gouged out his eyes and destroyed them.'[7]

The quoted lines in this fragment refer to Oedipus as the son of Polybus (the ruler of Corinth who brought up Oedipus as his son), meaning he is blinded before the discovery of his identity, and the servants of Laius presumably carry this out as a punishment for his killing of their master. In all, six plays entitled *Oedipus* are known to have been written in the fifth century BCE and there was also a version of the story in which Oedipus, before he ever came to Thebes, was blinded by his adoptive father, when he learned of the prophecy that Oedipus would kill his father.

Greek tragedies are nearly always based on some story about the distant past that would be familiar in some form or other to the original audience but there was no telling how a new presentation of this story would be handled by the dramatist.[8] An analogy may be made with a modern audience watching a new Western about Billy the Kid: knowing that he will be killed and that Pat Garrett will be responsible for his death paradoxically creates the audience's sense of a drama waiting to be enjoyed, for everything depends on how the known story will be told. With Greek tragedy, the dramatist is aware of what his audience knows about a particular story and can choose to alter a version as he wishes. This gives the playwright considerable creative space in which to work and a correlative to this is that an audience would watch a drama in the full expectation of there being something new to see about a familiar story. The fact that Sophocles' play begins many years after he has killed his father and married his mother may well have been the first of many dramatic surprises awaiting the audience. Similarly, given that there is no mention before Sophocles' play that Oedipus himself received an oracle at Delphi predicting he would kill his father and marry his mother, it may also have been a revelation for the audience to hear Oedipus refer to this oracle (line 791).

Democracy and tragedy

Tragedy developed in Athens alongside the birth and development of democracy. When Thespis, the legendary founder of tragedy, was said to have won the inaugural competition in tragedy in Athens in 534 (only some forty years before the birth of Sophocles) the city was ruled by the tyrant Pisistratus. Less than thirty years later and little more than a decade before Sophocles was born, the reforms of Cleisthenes had marked a crucial step in the transfer of power from a group of aristocratic families to a far larger citizen body of adult males in Athens. A possible return to tyranny haunted the fledgling democracy and the practice of ostracism, voting to expel for ten years a citizen deemed too powerful for the good of the *polis*, was one measure used to keep this threat at bay.

When *Oedipus* was performed for the first time in Athens it is possible that up to half of the total number of adult male citizens (citizenship was restricted to those whose parents were both native-born Athenians) were in attendance. It is thought that the population of Attica at this time amounted to about a quarter of a million but this included women, children, slaves and resident foreigners, none of whom were entitled to attend or vote at the Assembly when the *dēmos* met on the Pnyx Hill, very close to the theatre. It is debatable if women were allowed to attend theatrical performances but male non-citizens could make up part of an audience.

Theatre was part of Athenian life in a way that has no modern parallel and it cannot easily be separated from the city's development of a participatory democracy, a form of government which it is equally hard to find a parallel for in the modern world even if the imperialism, patriarchy and xenophobia which also characterized it has been ably and amply imitated. In Athens, for example, special financial provision was made to enable even the poorest citizens to pay the ticket price (equivalent to a day's wage for an unskilled man) for entry to the theatre. It is not known whether this Theoric Fund existed during Sophocles' time but the principle of using public funds for participation in political events was in operation from the 450s when a small payment was introduced for jury attendance and active military service.

Interpreting the play within the context of late fifth-century Athens affects the understanding of many aspects of the drama, including the date of its first production. There is no conclusive evidence of the actual year but following the outbreak of the Peloponnesian War in 431 a series of plagues affected Athens and, given that the pre-Sophoclean Oedipus myth does not mention a plague, it could be argued that this is the background for the one in *Oedipus*.[9] In addition to plague, the blight on crops mentioned at the start of the drama (25, 171) could be echoing the annual invasions of Attica by Peloponnesian armies which saw the burning of crops and cutting down of olive trees. Thucydides, witnessing what took place, recorded the disaster: 'Such was the affliction which had come on the Athenians and was pressing them hard – people dying inside the city, and the devastation of their land outside.'[10] The war would explain why a chorus of Theban elders praying for the lifting of the plague call for the defeat of Ares (190), the 'unhonoured' (215) god of war whom they call on Zeus to destroy (202). Ares as the patron god of Thebes and unassociated with plague would hardly be condemned like this, so an argument runs, unless the Theban identity of the chorus has been displaced by a more urgent memory of the situation affecting Athens. Building on this, Bernard Knox thinks the call to the gods to 'come to us now, if ever before, when ruin rushed upon the state, you drove destruction's flame away out of our land' (164–165) makes sense in terms of the especially terrible plague which returned in 427/426. Allied to possible parodic references to *Oedipus* in a comedy by Aristophanes produced in 424, Knox pins down Sophocles' play to the year 425.[11] But there is no conclusive evidence for this and Oliver Taplin, arguing from fundamental differences between comedy and tragedy in respect of topical references – 'Most tragedy casts its spell in a more exclusive, almost hypnotic way; to be effective it demands the total concentration of its audience, intellectual and emotional. Explicit self-reference breaks the spell' – comes to an opposite conclusion: 'In other words, I suggest that, for example, the only years which we can exclude with confidence as the date for the first performance of *Oedipus Tyrannos* were the years of the plague.'[12]

The influence of the social and political background on Sophocles' play can go beyond the empirical to a more complex understanding of how Athenian drama mediated antagonisms and tensions within the *polis*. In the case of *Oedipus*, the play has been seen to reflect the body politic by way of a correspondence between the presentation of Oedipus and the figure of Pericles, the leading politician and statesman of Athens until he died from the plague in 429. For the historian Thucydides, a contemporary of Pericles and Sophocles, Pericles was the 'first of citizens', echoing the chorus' view of Oedipus as the 'first of men' (32), embodying the ideology of Athens. In his funeral oration for the war dead at the end of the first year of the Peloponnesian War, Pericles gives voice to the self-image of his city and in his funeral speech, as recorded by Thucydides, he singles out the Athenian qualities which have made the city what it is. Athenians, he says, are decisive and they make things happen through the force of their will and intellect, combining daring with deliberation – 'whereas with others their courage relies on ignorance, and for them to deliberate is to hesitate'.[13]

There are obvious similarities with the character of Oedipus, but as Bernard Knox puts it, the correspondence need not be taken as a conscious one:

> All this does not necessarily mean that Sophocles' audience drew a conscious parallel between Oedipus and Athens (or even that Sophocles himself did); what is important is that they could have seen in Oedipus a man endowed with the temperament and talents they prized most highly in their own democratic leaders and in their ideal vision of themselves. Oedipus the King is a dramatic embodiment of the creative vigor and intellectual daring of the fifth-century Athenian spirit.[14]

If there was some intuitive recognition by the audience of *themselves* in Oedipus, then it was not an altogether comforting one given that the 'creative vigor' and 'intellectual daring' has as its obverse an ultra-rationalist self-belief that may backfire to disastrous effect. The sophists of Athens, in the minds of some, became associated with just such an overly confident belief in the powers of reason, especially when time-honoured religious beliefs were questioned. Sophists were regarded with suspicion by conservative-minded traditionalists who feared that if rationalism was employed to subvert long-established beliefs and practices like divine foreknowledge and oracles, then the very fabric of society was in danger of being torn apart. An issue like this can be seen as an undercurrent in the play, as when Jocasta 'proves' how a prophecy can be mistaken (707ff., 848ff.) and the alarmed chorus responds by reaffirming its belief in the gods. Never, they say, can they piously attend oracular shrines if divine predictions are disproved. The chorus calls on Zeus to see what is happening and take some action:

> O Zeus, if you are rightly called
> the sovereign lord, all-mastering,
> let this not escape you nor your ever-living power!
> The oracles concerning Laius
> are old and dim and men regard them not.
> Apollo is nowhere clear in honour; God's service perishes.
>
> (896–910)

If the authority of the gods is to be preserved it follows that the divine predictions reported by Jocasta and Oedipus, however dire, *should* be fulfilled and when this is seen to be the case the qualities of mind that Oedipus so confidently embodied are reduced to dust. He was a questioner, an investigator, the absolute rationalist who pounces on a numerical discrepancy, that between a reported plurality of bandits at the crossroads and the singular indubitable presence of himself, to exclaim self-evidently that one cannot be the same as many (842ff.). It turns out that one can be the same as many if accounts by more than one person are compared and a mistake is seen to have occurred. This allows for the play to be seen as a criticism of the hyper-rationalism that conservative Athenians alleged to be circulating in what they saw as sophist-influenced quarters of the city: 'The play then is a tremendous reassertion of the traditional religious view that man is ignorant, that knowledge belongs only to the gods.'[15]

Democracy arrived quickly in Athens and gave body to the individual's responsibility for his action, but the city's roots lay in an ancient past where gods could govern all or any aspect of life. This allows for a view of tragedy as a dramatic form that reflects the tension between these two cultures, a view associated with Jean-Pierre Vernant (1914–2007):

> The tragic turning point thus occurs when a gap develops at the heart of the social experience. It is wide enough for the oppositions between legal and political thought on the one hand and the mythical and heroic traditions on the other to stand out quite clearly. Yet it is narrow enough for the conflict in values still to be a painful one and for the clash to continue to take

place. A similar situation obtains with regard to the problems of human responsibility that arise as a hesitant progress is made toward the establishment of law. The tragic consciousness of responsibility appears when the human and divine levels are sufficiently distinct for them to be opposed while still appearing to be inseparable. The tragic sense of responsibility emerges when human action becomes the object of reflection and debate while still not being regarded as sufficiently autonomous to be fully self-sufficient.[16]

Thus we have Oedipus struggling to make rational sense of his world but at the same time enmeshed in the web of divine fore-knowledge and in this way *Oedipus* is seen to reflect tensions within the Athenian *polis* as it develops its democracy.

A male citizen of Athens enacted his legal civic identity as a juror chosen by lot for court cases and his political identity by casting his vote in the Assembly while the sense of a citizen collective found expression in public festivals. And one of the most important festivals that took place in Athens, dedicated to the god Dionysus and thus called the City Dionysia, occurred annually in the spring and lasted for nearly a week. It was a sacred event and featured ritualistic practices that included a procession, commemorating the arrival of Dionysus in Athens, that featured the carrying of an icon of Dionysus (a mask on a wooden pole decorated with a costume and ivy) from the theatre named after him, situated below the Acropolis on its south-east slopes. This procession arrived at an olive grove outside the city, known as the Academy and situated on the road that tradition held Dionysus to have taken when he first came to the city. After resting at the Academy overnight the procession returned with the icon to the theatre. The purpose-built Theatre of Dionysus was first constructed around 500 and it was here, as a part of the festival, that men and boys competed in the singing of dithyrambs and the performing of the dramas of three tragedians.

The dramatic performances were experienced as a celebration of a communal identity. In the broadest sense possible the City Dionysia and the performance of plays were political and this makes it all the more astonishing that a play like *Oedipus*, looking directly into a heart of darkness and confronting deeply held taboos, was acted out in the full light of day for the citizen body of Athens. Such dramatic performances probed issues that lay under the public surface of a small city's life where family counted for so much. Tragedy was the city's unconscious – a domain where parents could be killed by their children, sons sleep with their mothers and searches for the truth lead to the uncovering of dark, repressed secrets – and this makes it even more remarkable that tragedies were performed in what today would be called a nationalized theatre.

In preparation for the annual City Dionysia playwrights submitted a set consisting of three tragedies and a less serious satyr play, the latter named after the playful, mythical creatures who accompanied Dionysus, to a senior official of the city called the *archōn eponymous*. This would take place months before the festival but it is not known whether the texts had to be complete at this stage; nor is it known how a decision was reached as to which three playwrights would be successful in having their sets chosen for performance. The tragedians who were selected were allocated actors, chorus members and their *chorēgos*, a wealthy individual who financed the costs of a tragedy's chorus, while all other costs were funded by the city.

The first of a dramatist's three tragedies began early in the morning and performances followed one another, concluding with the satyr play. Comedies were most probably performed in the same theatre on another day. Audiences were large, estimates vary from 6,000 to 17,000 (out of a total of around 30,000 adult male citizens), and prizes were awarded by a group of judges (selected by lot) for the best, second-best and third-best of the twelve different tragedies and satyr plays.[17] Prizes were also awarded to actors and *chorēgoi* and it is possible that the quality of a tragedy's production was a factor in the award of prizes to a dramatist.

A sense of the sacred

It has been forcefully argued by Oliver Taplin that just because Greek tragedies were performed as part of a religious festival involving ritual elements it does not follow that such rituals influenced the form of the genre:

> The plays were performed within the sacred area of Dionysus, in the presence of the priest, and were preceded and followed by fixed rituals. All true. But the fact is that these circumstances

have left no trace whatsoever on the tragedies themselves, no trace of the Dionysiac occasion, the time of year, the priests, the surrounding rituals, nothing. We could not tell one single thing about the Festival from the *internal* evidence of the plays; it is all supplied by external evidence.[18]

This itself may be 'all true' but a sense of the sacred and the felt influence of the divine in human affairs informs the religious dimension of the City Dionysia and finds expression in the tragedies that were performed there in honour of the god – and this is dramatically evident in the opening of *Oedipus*. An altar (*thymele*) stood in the middle of the theatre's acting area and the play begins with a delegation of Thebans positioned around this altar, on which are placed some of the olive branches twined with wool which they have carried with them to the palace. The branches are offerings to Apollo, the god of healing, and the Thebans have come as suppliants to petition their king. Supplication (*hiketeia*) is a ritual act in ancient Greek culture and occurs both in the world of the divine (the *Iliad* begins with the mother of Achilles, a goddess, supplicating Zeus on behalf of her son) and of the human (at the end of the *Iliad*, Priam, the father of slain Hector, supplicates Achilles to release the corpse of his son for burial). There is the smell of smoke rising from incense burnt on city altars as offerings to the god and the sound of special chants, paeans, to Apollo (*paianōn*, 5). The man who steps forth as the representative of the Thebans identifies himself as a priest of Zeus and solicits help from Oedipus, not just as king but as someone who could only have defeated the Sphinx with the assistance of a god (*prosthēkē theou*, 38).

When Creon first appears on the stage, having returned from his mission to Delphi, his whole body appears as if imbued with the divine spirit of Apollo and his oracular shrine at Delphi:

Oedipus: Lord Apollo, look at him – his head is crowned with laurel, his eyes glitter.
Let his words blaze, blaze like his eyes, and save us.
Priest: He looks calm, radiant, like a god. If he brought bad news, would he be wearing that crown of sparkling leaves?

(80–83, Berg and Clay)

There were a number of oracular sites in the Greek world, where a question could be put by an individual or a *polis* to a god and an answer received. The evidence suggests that most questions related to matters of cult practice or quotidian affairs, queries where a simple yes or no was deemed a satisfactory answer. The most important and prestigious oracular shrine in the ancient Greek world was at Delphi, a site regarded as the centre of the world. An inquirer visiting Delphi put his question to the priests and after due ceremony it was passed on to the *pythia*, a woman who in a trance-like state and seated on a tripod was able to communicate with the god Apollo and receive a response to the question.

The news that Creon brings is not as joyful as had been anticipated. It speaks of pollution and the strict terms required for its expiation. Birth, death, homicide, sacrilege and madness were the usual foci for the Greek concept of pollution, acts that rendered the person concerned a polluter and requiring a course of action to cleanse them. Pollution (*miasma*) for the ancient Greeks was regarded a material force, something so palpable as to be transmittable by physical contact (a court for murder trials in Athens was always roofless for this reason), and homicide and sacrilege created serious pollutions which in extreme cases could afflict the whole community.[19] This, according to Creon, is what the Delphic oracle confirms: the plague is an aspect of the pollution caused by the shedding of Laius' blood, the former king, and the pollution can only be removed by avenging those responsible for his death (107). This is the context for the curse that Oedipus places on whoever killed Laius and which reverberates throughout the play. Curses were an aspect of ancient Greek culture and one form they took in everyday life is evidenced by the curse tablets (*katadesmos*), sheets of lead inscribed with various maledictions, that private individuals used in the hope of influencing the affairs of others. Sometimes these tablets referred to spirits of the dead and were placed in graves or sanctuaries. Public curses were imprecations on behalf of a community, with legalistic as well as religious overtones, and it is this solemn type that Oedipus so religiously pronounces (246–248). Its significance is repeatedly evoked during the course of the drama, first by Teiresias when he warns the king 'faithfully to keep the letter of your proclamation' (350), later by

Oedipus himself when he realizes he may be the killer – 'O God, I think I have called curses on myself in ignorance' (744–745) – and then a second time:

> And it is I,
> I and no other have so cursed myself.
> And I pollute the bed of him I killed
> by the hands that killed him. Was I not born evil?
> Am I not utterly unclean?
>
> (820–823)

Oedipus is the pollution and he chooses to make public his identity as such when he comes out from the palace after having blinded himself. He asks to be sent away, as his own curse on the killer of Laius decreed, and calls himself 'accursed' (*kataratotaton*, 1345) and 'godless' (*atheos*, 1360). In spite, or because, of this profound alienation he feels there is now some special quality attached to his being: 'Yet I know this much: no sickness and no other thing will kill me' (1456). It is not that he thinks of himself as immortal but he does feel that his life must now take a certain course regardless of his wishes – although he looks to spending the rest of his time on Cithaeron, the mountain where his parents had intended him to perish as an infant. This sense of some unique attribute now belonging to him lies behind his reassurance to the chorus that there is no risk of pollution to themselves through physical contact with him.

> Approach and deign to touch me
> for all my wretchedness, and do not fear.
> No man but I can bear my evil doom
>
> (1414–1415)

What gives him this uniqueness belongs to the domain of the sacred and Creon grants it some degree of recognition when he looks on the blinded Oedipus for the first time and refers to him as 'this cursed, naked, holy thing' (*toiond' agos akalupton houtō deiknunai*, 1426–1427). This translation by Berg and Clay captures the ambiguity of the Greek term *agos*: 'For the Greek, the sacred is both holy and cursed, awful and dangerous, pure and polluted.'[20]

It is correct to point to an ambivalent relationship between pollution and the sacred in ancient Greek thought for while in many obvious ways they do function as diametrically opposed, as in the observance of rigid rules governing contact between temple priests and priestesses and someone affected by pollution, there is also a strange convergence whereby the polluted person is invested with a supernatural power, a negative blessing: 'This is why *agos* and *enagēs* [accursed], words that appear to be related to a root †*hag* conveying the idea of sacredness, to some extent overlap in usage with *miasma* [pollution].'[21]

The power of the gods to influence the affairs of Thebes is the subject of the first ode sung by the chorus (151–215), calling upon them for assistance by name – Athena, Artemis, Apollo, Bacchus, Zeus – while singling out dreadful Ares, the god of war, as the personification of the plague that so afflicts them. It is also noteworthy that Jocasta, although she makes disparaging remarks about the veracity of oracles, turns to Apollo when alarmed by the state of Oedipus' mind. She appears carrying garlands and prays to the god who is 'close to my life' (919, Berg and Clay). The Greeks knew too that the proximity to humans of the gods could take a demonic form, as when the servant is describing Oedipus' final rage when he searched for Jocasta in the palace and 'in his frenzy, a power above man was his guide; for 'twas none of us mortals who were nigh' (1258–1259, Jebb).

Notes

1 All dates are BCE unless otherwise indicated.

2 Quoted in Carey (2009), p. 260.

3 Lattimore (1967), p. 175 (11.271–280).

4 Lattimore (1969), p. 468 (23.679).

5 Sommerstein (2010), pp. 214–219.

6 For an account of Euripides' *Oedipus* see Macintosh (2009), pp. 20–24.

7 Quoted from Ahl (2008), p. 72.

8 'It's quite legitimate to take a play and treat it in a context which is closer to our experience. After all, that's exactly what Sophocles was

doing. He was using an old legend anyway, and making it modern.' Derek Walcott, quoted from Hall (2010), p. 328.

9 As pointed out by Edith Hall, however, it needs to be remembered that 'the earliest and greatest work of Greek literature, the *Iliad*, likewise opens with a plague sent by Apollo'. Hall (2008), p. xiv.

10 Thucydides (2009), p. 99 (2.54).

11 Knox (1979), pp. 112–124. There is also a case for a date around 429: see Newton (1980), pp. 5–22, and Janko (1999), pp. 15–19.

12 Taplin (1986), p. 171, p. 167.

13 Thucydides (2009), p. 93 (2.40).

14 Knox (2007), pp. 78–79.

15 Knox (1984), p. 152.

16 Vernant (1988), p. 27.

17 Ten judges cast their votes for prizes but only five votes, drawn by lottery, actually counted. This may have been an anti-corruption device for there was no way of knowing which of the ten judges' votes would come into play: 'You could bribe seven people and still lose; and you would never know if you got the votes you paid for'. Ahl (2008), p. 94.

18 Taplin (1983), pp. 3–4.

19 'What disturbs and distances the modern reader in the case both of Hercules [who, induced by a goddess, kills his own children in a state of madness] and Oedipus is the intensity of the pollution that emanates from an unintentional act.' Parker (1983), p. 317.

20 Burian and Shapiro (2011), p. 299.

21 Hornblower and Spawforth (1998), p. 553.

CHAPTER TWO

Form, language and style

Greek tragedy

If Greek mythology is understood as a way of thinking, an audaciously imaginative leap of the intellect was taken when instead of just reciting or referring to mythical stories someone took on the identity of one of the characters and spoke as that person. A shadowy figure called Thespis is credited with this bold innovation, sometime in the 530s. Thespis was a singer of dithyrambs, song-and-dance compositions honouring Dionysus, performed by choruses of fifty men and boys and which, it is supposed, included a narrative element. He seems to have been an itinerant, masked performer who presumably realized he could enliven a performance by adopting the persona of a mythical character. The grounds for such a theatrical move were prefigured by passages of direct speech in epic recitation and when a passage was a particularly long one there must have been moments when the bard as performer segued into a role-playing actor.

Religious rituals involving groups of singers and dancers may have facilitated the development of mimetic gestures on the part of these groups and, if so, such a development would have influenced the emergence of the role of the chorus in Greek tragedy. The word *tragoidia* may be related to the word for a goat, *tragos*, and to the word *oidos* which means a song, but if this is the case it cannot be known for sure if it relates back to a festive event featuring the sacrifice of a goat, or to a chorus dressed as goats or in goatskins or to something else again. That the origins of tragedy are bound up with an event involving a chorus would seem to be supported by the view that the sense of the Greek word for actor, *hypokritēs*, is 'the one who answers or responds', and which perhaps harks back to some seminal moment when a member of a choral group took on the role of someone from a myth.[1] Whether and how this might relate to someone called Thespis cannot be known but somehow, out of the singing of dithyrambs, religious rituals and choral singers and dancers the form of tragedy developed and in its evolution the playwright (*poiētēs*, Greek for 'maker'), the tragedian, emerged.

The chief actor of a tragedy was the *protagonistes* and at some stage a second actor was introduced, though by the time of Sophocles it was common to have three actors. According to Aristotle, it was the tragedian Aeschylus who introduced a second actor and Sophocles who first brought in a third one. The titular role in *Oedipus* would have been played by the *protagonistes*, with the other two actors sharing the various remaining roles so that the actor playing Creon also took the part of the Corinthian messenger and the actor of Jocasta also played the part of the herdsman. There were also silent actors for non-speaking parts like attendants and in the case of *Oedipus* the two children who appear at the end of the drama. There was a formal stage dress for characters in a Greek tragedy, marked by an elaborate patterning and loose sleeves.

A playwright's three plays could deal with the same story or the subject matter could be different for each play. In the case of *Oedipus*, nothing is known about the other two tragedies or the satyr play which completed its set. *Oedipus at Colonus*, which deals with the end of Oedipus' life, was produced posthumously in 401, many years after *Oedipus* and not as part of a trilogy dealing with the same story. *Antigone*, another play by Sophocles, was produced a number of years before *Oedipus* but deals with events later in the time of the myth when Oedipus' daughter, Antigone, has grown up. The notion of a Theban 'cycle' of plays, a Theban 'trilogy', can easily give the mistaken impression that Sophocles conceived of *Oedipus*, *Antigone* and *Oedipus at Colonus* as a cohesive set, ignoring the fact that in *Antigone* Oedipus has already died while in *Oedipus at Colonus* he is alive.

There are a number of significant differences between modern theatre and the form in which tragic drama was invented in

Athens. All acting parts were taken by males and it may have been the case, though the evidence is inconclusive, that women did not even form part of the audience. The theatre was open-air, no lighting was necessary, and its site still stands in Athens although nothing survives of the original wooden structure; a stone-built theatre replaced it in the late fourth century and this was rebuilt more than once in the centuries that followed. The circular acting area was backed by a low, probably wooden, structure known as the *skene* (hence our word scenery), about 4 metres high and 12 metres long; the practice of painting on the skene is attributed to Sophocles by Aristotle. The *skene* had a central doorway and possibly a smaller doorway on each side. It is possible, though this is not supported by the consensus of scholarly opinion, that a low-level platform stood in front of the *skene*. If such a platform existed it would have sloped or had steps down into the area called the *orchestra* – from the Greek word for dancing – where the chorus sang, danced and interacted with the three actors who between them took on the roles of a play's characters. The *orchestra*, the origins of which probably predate those of drama and lie with the circular floors fashioned out of a hillside and used for threshing corn, was about 20 metres in diameter and in its centre stood an altar (*thymele*).

The *skene* in *Oedipus* represents the palace of the king of Thebes and the play begins with Oedipus, the present king of the city, standing in front of it and addressing a group of citizens in the *orchestra*. It is uncertain how this group was represented and whether on this particular occasion some extras were employed. Of the two other actors available, one is required for the role of Creon who makes his appearance before the chorus. The term prologue in Greek tragedy covers all that takes place before the arrival of the chorus and in the plays of Aeschylus and Euripides the prologue is usually the work of a single character; Sophocles differs by preferring his dramas to begin with more than one character. Actors entered by ways of aisles known as eisodos or parodos, one from each side, and were visible to the audience as they made their way into the performance space. No stage directions are given in the extant texts and as those found in modern translations have been added by the editor, this sometimes becomes a critical issue. In the scene in *Oedipus* where Teiresias delivers his parting words (447–462), making explicit reference to Oedipus as the killer of Laius and the father of children born out of incest with his own mother, any director of the play needs to consider how these words are delivered, whether directly to Oedipus or out of his hearing as one or both of the characters exit the stage area.

After its arrival, the chorus, usually made up of around fifteen members, never leaves the *orchestra* and its singing of an ode is accompanied by music from the *aulos*, an oboe-like instrument, and dance steps. The little that is known about the dance steps, coming from paintings on vases, indicates that dancing was not an individual act and was performed as a ranked group. The first ode of the chorus is the parode while those that come after are called stasima (singular, stasimon). The two stanza-like parts of an ode, called the strophe and antistrophe, take their name from the Greek word for turning and refer to the dance-like movement of the chorus. The two parts of an ode have the same metre. Choral odes punctuate the different scenes of a Greek tragedy, allowing time for actors to change parts.

The wearing of masks is one of the major differences between Athenian and modern drama, although it is not known for sure how and why this tradition developed. Thespis was credited with the act of whitening his face with lead and using flowers to decorate it and some such preparation may have developed into the linen masks that were covered with painted plaster and fitted over the head of all actors by the fifth century. Masks covered the whole face and although none have survived, vase paintings suggest that the emphasis was on simplicity of expression.

Speech and song

There is a basic distinction to be made between the lyrics of choral odes sung to the accompaniment of music (and in a dialect that was not native to Athens) and scenes featuring dialogue between the non-choral actors. Scenes of spoken dialogue (soliloquies are extremely rare given that the chorus is nearly always present) can be divided into *rheseis*, set speeches where the lines are delivered without interruption, and a rapid exchange between characters of single lines known as *stichomythia*, or *distichmoyhtia* for double lines. An example of both of these is the long scene between Oedipus and Teiresias. Scenes featuring the rapid exchange of lines lend themselves to the build up of excitement when one of the characters is coming under pressure and the drama can be heightened by interjections from a third party, either another individual or the chorus, and by moments of physical contact. A particularly good example of this, with all the elements just mentioned being included, is the encounter between Oedipus and the herdsman (1120ff.). When half-lines are exchanged, as towards the end of the scene between Oedipus and Creon before the chorus announces the arrival of Jocasta (627ff.), this is called *antilabē*.

Greek tragedies are not as rigidly governed as these formal distinctions might suggest and the playwright is licensed to be flexible. Some lines by an individual actor can be delivered as a solo lyric or the leader of a chorus can be brought into a scene of spoken dialogue. It is not known for sure how rule-governed were the dancing motions of a chorus, even whether they primarily moved in circular patterns or in a more block-like and military-style fashion, and it is likely that variations were possible just as they were for the delivery of lines by non-choral actors. It is also possible that the lines of a chorus were accompanied by hand movements, signifiers in their own right and readily interpretable by discerning members of an audience.

The messenger speech (*angelia*) is the term for a set speech reporting a critical event that has taken place offstage, delivered by an *exangelos* if referring to something inside the *skene*, or by an *angelos* if reporting on an event at a distant location – another city or land or the countryside – and typically though not always occurring in the second half of the play. The usual format for a messenger speech, as in *Oedipus* when news of Jocasta's suicide is reported (1223ff.), is for the gist of the information to be delivered in a short dialogue before the messenger is requested to relate the news in more detail. Messenger speeches are a familiar part of a tragedy and audiences recognized them as such, looking forward to the occasion they provided for a lengthy and colourful description of a dramatic moment. They provided an opportunity for the actor to impress his audience with the dramatic force of his descriptions and, through passages in direct speech with the actor momentarily taking on the part of one of the characters in the offstage events, the emotional intensity of what is being reported.[2] What makes the messenger speech in *Oedipus* unique is that the messenger does *not* use direct speech, relying on paraphrases rather than direct verbal re-enactment, such is the appalling nature of the narrative he reports.

Greek tragedies are written in verse form and based on patterns of long and short syllables rather than the stressed and unstressed arrangements of sound in English verse. Despite this difference both languages employ various metres, especially the iambic and the anapaestic, which can be read as basically similar. Thus, the ordinary metre for speech in Athenian tragedy is the iambic trimester, with each line consisting of three units of two iambs (short–LONG syllables) and this alternating pattern bore some resemblance to the rhythm of everyday speech (as do patterns of unstressed and stressed syllables in the everyday speech of English).[3] While the parts of a tragedy that were sung by the chorus follow a strictly lyrical metre there is also a third type of metre that comes between the iambic trimester and the lyrical. This third type is an anapaestic rhythm (short–short–LONG) and this can lend itself to a jogging effect, hence the term 'marching' anapaests and a possible origin in the tramp of soldiers' feet. Such 'marching' anapaests characterize the chanted lines of a chorus, especially when first entering and finally leaving the *orchestra*, but the jogging effect of this kind of rhythm can be modulated and used as an index of a heightened, emotional register in the speaker. Known as the 'melic', this type of metre is used in spoken words that were possibly accompanied by music from the *aulos* and recited in a way that might have been closer to song than speech.

The metre indicates how a particular passage was delivered, whether sung or spoken, sung as a solo or duet or in an interchange with the chorus or sung and danced by the chorus. This will not be obvious to many readers using the Greek text and certainly cannot be known in the reading of a translation, but it can be important to make a basic distinction between sung and spoken lines. An advantage of some translations (see page 157) is that this distinction is made clear and the reader can register changes in the emotional intensity of a scene, as when Oedipus sings for the first time when he enters after blinding himself (1313ff.).

Aristotle

The Greek philosopher Aristotle (384–322 BCE), mentioned more than once already, is of tremendous importance in an understanding of Greek tragedy because of what has survived of his writings on the subject. His works on poetry that were admired most in ancient times have been lost, but what has survived is his *Poetics*, a set of notes that he wrote for his own use or for the benefit of his students. They contain an analysis of tragedy written not by a contemporary of Sophocles, but by someone who most probably would have attended theatrical productions after arriving in Athens from northern Greece at the age of seventeen to study in Plato's Academy. He later left Athens but returned in 335 to establish his own school, the Lyceum. As an intellectual who developed his own philosophy in the fourth century, Aristotle cannot be taken as representative of Greek thought or as someone writing topically and typically about the tragedies of playwrights like Sophocles. At the same time, given the two and a half millennia that separate our age from that of ancient Greece, he is closer in time and culture to the age that produced *Oedipus* than anyone else whose writings have survived. The most compelling reason for reading Aristotle's *Poetics* is the insights his analysis brings to bear on *Oedipus*, the play he singles out as being most representative of tragic drama, and why it continues to have such a hold over modern audiences and readers.

Aristotle defines tragedy as 'an imitation [*mimesis*] of an action . . . performed by actors, not through narration; effecting through pity and fear the purification [*katharsis*] of such emotions'.[4] His emphasis is on plot rather than poetry or character, tragedy 'is not an imitation of persons, but of actions and of life':

> Well-being and ill-being reside in action (*praxis*), and the goal of life is an activity, not a quality; people possess certain qualities in accordance with their character, but they achieve well-being or its opposite on the basis of how they fare. So the imitation of character is not the purpose of what the agents do; character is included along with and on account of the actions. So the events, i.e. the plot, are what tragedy is there for, and that is the most important thing of all.[5]

The course of an individual's life cannot simply be a function of the kind of person whose life it is. Someone can be ambitious and well-connected but this does not guarantee a successful rise in their chosen career for what determines the outcome is bound up with what the person does and the consequences; and this sense of action as the outcome is part of the Greek word *praxis*. The pity and fear evoked in tragedy are responses to the success ('well-being') or failure ('ill-being') attendant on the action and it follows therefore that plot, recording changes in fortune, is 'the most important of all'.

Two elements of plot identified by Aristotle as characteristic of tragedy are both exemplified by reference to *Oedipus*. One is *peripeteia* (reversal) and the example he gives is the messenger scene (924ff.): arriving with the good news that Oedipus will be the new king of Corinth, because his supposed father has died there, the messenger learns that Oedipus is reluctant to return out of fear of committing incest with his mother and he seeks to allay such a worry with facts about his infancy, facts that inexorably lead to Oedipus' discovery of his parricide and incest. *Peripeteia* is not a change in fortune *per se*, but a startling turnabout in events that brings about the opposite of what is expected. It is the paradox contained within the change in fortune that constitutes the reversal, not just the bare fact that a dramatic change of fortune has taken place.

The other important element in tragedy for Aristotle is *anagnonrisis* (recognition), 'a change from ignorance to knowledge, disclosing either a close relationship or enmity, on the part of people marked out for good or bad fortune' and for Aristotle, citing *Oedipus*, this works best when it occurs alongside a reversal.[6]

For Aristotle, feelings of pity and fear are aroused in an audience because the plot shows actions occurring in ways that are logical and yet contrary to expectation; there is a sense of astonishment at the course of events, especially when something uncanny happens, like the accident he refers to when 'the statue of Mitys in Argos killed the man who was responsible for Mitys' death by falling on top of him as he was looking at it. Things like that are not thought to occur at random.'[7] The unexpected change in events can in theory work in a positive direction and Greek tragedies may and do sometimes have happy endings, but for Aristotle the best kind of plots involve a change from good to bad fortune and this must be 'not due not to any moral defect or depravity, but to an error [*harmatia*] of some kind'.[8] *Harmatia*, coming from a word that also means missing the mark in archery, is not a flaw in character but a mistake, an error that proves to have terrible, unintended consequences.

Suffering is the consequences of *harmatia*, this is what causes the audience to experience pity and fear, and Aristotle sees an

intensifying of the tragic effect when it involves people closely connected (*philoi*): 'What one should look for are situations in which
sufferings arise within close relationships, e.g. brother kills brother,
son father, mother son, or son mother.'[9] He goes on from here to
observe that while playwrights cannot make fundamental changes
to a traditional story, they can make choices about how to use them
and he contrasts a play like Euripides' *Medea*, where Jason is punished for his infidelity by his wife's decision to kill their children,
with one like *Oedipus* where a terrible deed is committed in ignorance. A drama where dreadful action arises from ignorance is held
to be superior to those where there is full knowledge of the harmful
action, even though for Aristotle better still is action planned in
ignorance but, at the last moment, not carried out; what all these
situations have in common are events that involve suffering. An
audience feels pity for those on the receiving end of the suffering
and fear that the same thing could happen to them.

The feelings of pity and fear undergo *katharsis* as a result of
being enacted in the theatre, but it is difficult to know just what
is meant by this term because the word *katharsis* carries the sense
of a spiritual cleansing as well as a physical, purgative process. It
is tempting to think that what Aristotle had in mind is related to
his argument that imitation is innate in humans and that 'we take
delight in viewing the most accurate possible images of objects
which in themselves cause distress when we see them'.[10] The feeling of fear is mediated by experiencing the suffering through the
drama; it does not actually happen to us, but we come to know
that, given a particular set of circumstances, something similar
could happen to us for real. This emotional and intellectual knowledge that is arrived at through the safety net of a staged presentation with actors is cathartic.

The public and the private

Aristotle's statement that tragedy 'is not an imitation of persons,
but of actions and of life' makes plain a fundamental characteristic of Athenian tragedy that makes it different to modern concep-
tions of tragic drama. The difference was noted by Kierkegaard:
'The peculiarity of ancient tragedy is that the action does not
issue exclusively from character, that the action does not find its

sufficient explanation in subjective reflection and decision . . . [the chorus] indicates, as it were, the more which will not be absorbed in individuality.'[11] Kierkegaard recognizes the importance of the chorus in defining the nature of Athenian tragedy and, like the wearing of masks, the chorus is one of the more obvious differences between a modern understanding of naturalistic theatre and the performances of tragedy in fifth-century Athens.

The open-air setting and the large size of the Athenian theatre point to other differences in the way the actors and chorus communicated with their audiences: there is a huge difference between the levels of intimacy capable of being created by mises en scène in a darkened auditorium with subtle lighting effects and the effects being aimed at in the bright sunshine of the Athenian theatre with many thousands of spectators. The distance between the stage area in front of the *skene* and the furthest row of spectators was over 100 metres – four times the distance of Shakespeare's Globe – and this would have influenced aspects of the performance and made, for example, frontal delivery by the actors and chorus their unquestioned mode of speaking and singing.

It is important, however, not to reduce differences between modern theatre and Greek tragic drama to merely practical aspects like the climate or the numerical size of the audience. This kind of reasoning leads to thinking of the mask of Athenian tragedy in terms of practical convenience, so that its open mouth for auditory projection is seen as a primitive megaphone that allows the voice to be amplified up and across the open space of the theatre. Similarly, the mask's large-sized face becomes a functional device that allows spectators in the back seats to recognize the character on stage and/or it facilitates the taking on of multiple and differently gendered roles by one actor. These may all be valid observations but, as John Jones persuasively puts it, they miss the point:

> *Prosōpon*, the Greek word for mask, also means face, aspect, person and stage-figure (*persona*); we should allow mask and face to draw semantically close together, and then we should enrich the face far beyond our own conception, until it is able to embrace (as it did for Greeks from the time of Homer) the look of the man together with the truth about him.[12]

The mask is an aesthetic artefact that *declares* an identity rather than hiding one, but we have become so fluent in conceiving of the mask as a concealment of a deeper 'real' self that what is lost is the Greeks' understanding of it as essentially the being of the whole person. The linguistic and gestural space of Greek tragedy operates outside the kind of introspective, private mode that characterizes, say, a Shakespeare soliloquy: it is 'a theatre of public events' and the chorus 'exerting the pressure of being heard and witnessed upon the stage figures, is the constant visible symbol of this public world.'[13] This way of seeing the role of the chorus is what Kierkegaard meant by 'the more which will not be absorbed in individuality'; in other words, a correlate to the absence of privacy from the world of Athenian tragedy is the highly stylized, public reality of what takes place on the stage with the costumed actors wearing masks and the chorus nearly always present.

The public nature of Athenian tragedy does not mean that playwrights and audiences were unaware of or unresponsive to people's private feelings, to the domain of intimacy, and it might be thought Kierkegaard is putting it too strongly when he claims 'the ancient world did not have subjectivity fully self-conscious and reflective'.[14] What it does mean is that the theatre of Athenian tragedy did not allow for the presentation of the kind of self-analytic subjectivity that is built into our sense of what is possible on the stage. Like the theatre of Beckett and Brecht, there is a lack, a vacancy, of affect – or rather an absence of the mode for expressing affect that we have become accustomed to – and interiority is not probed but projected in ways that may sometimes seem mechanistic. What makes one aspect of *Oedipus* especially interesting is the way we see this convention of the genre being pushed to its limit when the traumatic impact of what is unfolding in public is seen to impinge on the private, as when Jocasta and Oedipus come to share moments of unguarded privacy and she speaks of men dreaming of sleeping with their mothers (988ff.).[15]

Notes

1 From another sense given to the word *hypokritēs*, 'one who interprets', the actor explained a complex myth.

2 For a good account of the messenger scene in general and in relation to *Oedipus*, see Barrett (2002).

3 'But when speech was introduced nature itself found the appropriate form of verse, iambic being the verse-form closest to speech. There is evidence of this: we speak iambics in conversation with each other very often, but rarely dactylic hexameters – and only when we depart from the normal conversational tone.' Aristotle (1996), p. 8.

4 Ibid., p. 10.

5 Ibid., p. 11.

6 Ibid., pp. 18–19.

7 Ibid., p. 17.

8 Ibid., p. 21.

9 Ibid., p. 23.

10 Ibid., p. 6.

11 Kierkegaard (1971), p. 141.

12 Jones (1980), p. 44.

13 Gould (2001), p. 84 and p. 89.

14 Kierkegaard (1971), p. 141.

15 Gould (2001), p. 84.

CHAPTER THREE

Overview of themes

Tragic action

The significance for an understanding of *Oedipus* of Aristotle's statement that tragedy 'is not an imitation of persons, but of actions and of life' is likely to be underrated by readers and spectators who are accustomed to the psychological verisimilitude that typifies so much of modern fiction. A concern with characters' rich interiorities, their inner feelings and reflections, their three dimensionality, is such a standard (and for many a sacred) hallmark of contemporary fiction that it may blind one to the contours of the tragic action in *Oedipus*. Consider the reversals that mark the course of events in the play: Oedipus is the ruler of Thebes, renowned for his success in outwitting the Sphinx by correctly answering her riddle but unable to lift the plague devastating his city. The oracle at Delphi is consulted and declares that the pestilence will end if the death of Laius is avenged (107). Oedipus sets about this task, places a solemn curse on those responsible and questions a blind seer who is provoked into mysteriously asserting that Oedipus himself is the killer being sought. In trying to calm matters his wife mentions how the former king died at a spot where three roads meet and this shocks Oedipus for he remembers an encounter there and realizes he may indeed be the killer. A herdsman is summoned who witnessed the encounter, but then a messenger arrives to report the death of Oedipus' supposed father in Corinth, good news that on the face of it invalidates an earlier oracle saying

Oedipus would kill his father. That oracle also said he would have sex with his mother so Oedipus is reluctant to return to Corinth, but the messenger is pleased to discount such a possibility. It was he who was given the infant Oedipus by a herdsman who had worked for the king of Thebes, whereupon he carried the infant to Corinth, where the king and queen adopted him. Jocasta, realizing the truth, begs Oedipus to cease his investigations, but he desists, thinking she is merely afraid he will be shown to have lowly origins. Now the herdsman arrives who witnessed the killing of the king, but he also happens to be the one who gave the infant Oedipus to the messenger and he knows the identity of the infant's real parents. 'I am on the brink of frightful speech', says the herdsman; 'And I of frightful hearing. But I must hear', replies Oedipus (1069–1070), now realizing he was the abandoned son of the king, that he killed him at the crossroads and then married his own mother in Thebes.

The important events have already occurred and the play's plot is the twists and turns that lead Oedipus to discover what has already taken place. Seeking to help his city, his action in summoning and cross-examining witnesses unwittingly uncovers a past that could have stayed hidden. What appears as a perverse series of circumstances led to the events that are uncovered and, similarly, an unintended and unfortunate set of moments turn the proceedings of Oedipus' investigation into a nightmarish journey of self-discovery. A part of the perverseness that infects the plot is the sense of Oedipus unintentionally helping to bring about his own tragedy. After all, he left Corinth in the first place because he wanted to establish the truth of his parentage after a drunk said he was illegitimate (780).

Essential to the tragic action is the fact that Oedipus discovers he has done something truly awful and even though he acted in ignorance he knows he cannot just ignore the knowledge that has come to him. Bernard Williams is right to insist that Oedipus' knowledge of the act itself carries its own tremendous weight, regardless of motive or lack of it:

> The whole of the *Oedipus Tyrannus*, that dreadful machine, moves to the discovery of just one thing, that *he did it*. Do we understand the terror of that discovery only because we residually share magical beliefs in blood-guilt, or archaic notions

of responsibility? Certainly not: we understand it because we know that in the story of one's life there is an authority exercised by what one has done, and not merely by what one has intentionally done.[1]

Oedipus can be polluted but without being guilty and this is the frame of understanding that informs the theme of knowledge and self-knowledge in *Oedipus*.

Knowledge and self-knowledge

The uncertainty of self-knowledge moves restlessly through *Oedipus* and creates disturbing currents of thought. There is a story from Iceland about a thief, Arnes Pálsson, who in 1756 cleverly managed to escape being caught by joining the posse hunting for him on Mt Akrafjall; this kind of ingenuity is not available to Oedipus because he lacks the knowledge that he is the person being searched for and – such ingenuity as there is proving peculiarly reflexive – the search is initiated and relentlessly sustained by himself alone. He is looking for himself but without the knowledge that enabled Arnes Pálsson to be both hunter and hunted, and it is this lack of awareness that directs the course of Sophocles' tragic drama.

Oedipus is in many ways the opposite of whom he took himself to be. He arrives as a stranger from Corinth but actually he is a Theban returning to the city where he was born; as a tyrant (*tyrannus*) he cannot consider himself the legitimate ruler of Thebes but in fact he is; the solver of the Sphinx's riddle, he fails to decipher the riddling prophecy of Delphi concerning his parents; the judge who passes judgement on the killer of Laius is himself the criminal; the man who would save Thebes from the plague is the source of the affliction; the 'first of men' (33) ends by asking who could be more miserable than himself (1204). And there is the post-*Oedipus* irony that the term Oedipus complex, originating as it does from Sophocles' play, cannot be applied to someone who, without knowing their relationship to him, accidentally happens to kill his father and have sex with his mother.

Oedipus is not an arrogant or stupidly self-conceited person and only under provocation from a taunting Teiresias does he express pride in the intelligence that saw him outwit the Sphinx, a half-woman and half-lion quadruped, described by the Latin author Hygines as the poser of a deadly challenge to the Theban community:[2]

> The Sphinx, offspring of Typhon, was sent into Boeotia, and was laying waste the fields of the Thebans. She proposed a contest to Creon, that if anyone interpreted the riddle which she gave, she would depart, but that she would destroy whoever failed, and under no other circumstances would she leave the country. When the King heard this, he made a proclamation throughout Greece. He promised that he would give the kingdom and his sister Jocasta in marriage to the person solving the riddle of the Sphinx. Many came out of greed for the kingdom, and were devoured by the Sphinx, but Oedipus, son of Laius, came and interpreted the riddle. The Sphinx leaped to her death.[3]

Oedipus, at the start of the play is a highly respected and self-assured king and yet within the course of an hour or so the fabric of his life inexorably unravels and, like the Sphinx, he is ruined by an answer to a riddle, in this case the enigma that was his life. When this riddle is answered the consequences are horrific. A messenger describes what happened inside the palace when Oedipus searched for his wife with murderous intent and, having found her self-slain, took a brooch from her garment and blinded himself. When he comes out from the palace to face the public world the audience is prepared for the spectacle of an utterly broken man, sightless because of what he has learned about himself. Yet Oedipus has not been utterly destroyed by his self-knowledge and, contrary to what the chorus expects, chooses to remain alive. He defends his act of self-blinding and is ready to go on living, no longer in a state of ignorance about his identity, bringing to some kind of conclusion the word play that surrounds his name.

The name Oedipus (Oidipous) may come from the Greek root –*id* (with forms of *eid*- and *oid*-) which means both to 'see' and to 'know', reflecting the fact that our basis for knowledge is the phenomenal world around us, a world that we intuit through our senses. The philosophical primacy of this is addressed by Kant in the first sentence of the introduction to his *Critique of Pure Reason* when he asserts that there 'can be no doubt that all our knowledge begins with experience'.[4] The *Critique* goes on to argue that the mind makes an order of the phenomenal, the knowable physical world of appearances, by transforming what it intuits with concepts of the understanding, forms of thought that Kant calls 'categories'. Such categories, an example of which is the concept of cause, possess a truth that is presupposed. Without these forms of thought, Kant states, the world would not be intelligible to us: 'they relate of necessity and *a priori* to the objects of experience, for the reason that only by means of them can any object whatsoever of experience be thought'.[5] It follows for Kant that any object encountered through our senses must have a cause, even if in a particular case the cause may not be known to us, because this is an *a priori* condition, a 'transcendental' condition of the experience of objects. These categories of thought are not generated through a process of abstraction based on our experiences, but spontaneously by our understanding. This is how our reasoning works and, to return to Sophocles' drama, the power of reasoning is what makes Oedipus the kind of person he is. It was through a process of reasoning that he was able to answer the Sphinx's riddle and, when the oracle at Delphi links finding who killed Laius with the pollution that threatens to destroy Thebes, his investigation into the unsolved death proceeds in the same way. When this line of inquiry leads to questions about his own identity, Oedipus continues to apply his rational powers of understanding until he finally reaches the truth. He is driven by the necessity of desire and must do what he does if he is to be who he is. It is not the force of his will that drives him to find out who killed Laius but the non-negotiable force of his own being, his commitment to confronting the truth.

Left at this, we have an ontologically complete account of the world and our knowledge of it; but Kant, like Sophocles, is not content with such a gratifyingly consistent account of the world. Kant distinguishes two distinct orders of reality, the phenomenal and the noumenal, and the consequent difference between things in themselves and things as they appear to us. Our senses provide us with something about the world outside of ourselves but it does not follow that what we intuit is a pure and unqualified awareness of whatever it is that causes our senses to experience something in the first place. For Kant, there is an order of being that our rationality cannot access and while Sophocles is not writing a philosophical treatise – there is no intention to try and force a correspondence between ideas in his play and Kant's epistemology – questions about knowledge are raised by *Oedipus* and it is worth drawing attention to the philosophical nature of the debate. It is the case that Sophocles' drama unfolds a sense of there being more to reality than just the dimension of the phenomenal and our understanding of it in rational thought. This is not the noumenal in Kant's sense of the term, but in the ancient Greek world, expressed partly through omens and prophecies, acknowledgement is paid to forces over and above the merely human. Oedipus thought he knew how to go about understanding his world but comes to realize that his intelligence could never have prepared him for what was always known by Apollo and uttered at Delphi:

> All life moves within a shell-like containment of final ignorance and impotence. To act or think in self-founded certainty of what tomorrow will bring is to ape the poor blind madman who throws away his stick, shakes off the guiding hand and plunges forward alone.[6]

The etymology that relates Oedipus' name to the sense of sight is confirmation of the importance that is attached to terms of seeing and not seeing, sight and blindness, that run throughout the play. Oedipus thinks he has the ability to see clearly and sets about uncovering what has remained hidden while Teiresias is blind but he can 'see' the truth and does not wish to reveal what has remained hidden; at the end of the play Oedipus is blind and his 'blindness strikes at the terms of his claims to knowledge and insight'.[7]

The bringing into light of what was previously invisible to most of those involved begins in the play with the Delphic oracle speaking of a remedy for the plague. Other oracles speak of what will come to pass, and essential elements in the fulfilment of these prophecies rely on the spoken word: the words of the drunk in Corinth prompt Oedipus to visit Delphi and the words he hear there take him away from Corinth and on to the crossroads; his own words that answer the Sphinx's riddle lead to Oedipus marrying Jocasta. The investigations by Oedipus are all conducted verbally and they culminate in a climactic scene with the herdsman and its series of speech acts (1110ff.): questions, orders, counter-orders, threats, rebukes, refusals, assertions, pleadings, admissions and regrets.[8] The spoken word, language, seems bound up with the process of attaining a state of knowledge. Oedipus conducts himself on such an assumption: when Creon returns from Delphi, but hesitates to report what happened in front of the Theban citizens, Oedipus instructs him to speak publicly (*es pantas audau*, 93). Jocasta is just as much a positivist when it comes to the value of the spoken word: when she recalls how the herdsman spoke of robbers at the crossroads (842), not a solitary assassin, and Oedipus wants him summoned to the palace to confirm the discrepancy, she insists that the herdsman 'cannot unsay it now' (849). Words from the domain of the secular are invested with an immutability that properly belongs only to the sacred realm of oracles and prophecies.

Counter-currents of silence and evasion complicate the means whereby language can be expected to advance a state of knowledge. Oedipus asks the oracle who his parents are but is not given an answer, being told instead that he will commit parricide and incest (though this is a kind of riddling answer to the question because his discovery of who his parents are comes about as a [long-delayed] consequence of his parricide and incest). The oracle consulted about the plague says that the death of Laius be avenged, but the matter of who is culpable is left open. Oedipus, enraged by Teiresias' refusal to give a straight answer to questions, asks him if he is reckless enough to continue his evasions:

> Oedipus: Do you imagine you can always talk
> like this, and live to laugh at it hereafter?
> Teiresias: Yes, if the truth has anything of strength.
>
> (368–369)

Oedipus' reply is that the blind seer has neither physical nor mental strength – 'you are blind in mind and ears as well as in your eyes' – but it is he who is blind to the knowledge Teiresias possesses, a knowledge that is delivered in such riddling language that the scene comes to an end with Oedipus reduced to silence.

It can be argued that the play's explorations into the nature of knowledge leads to a reaffirmation of a traditional belief in the power of the gods and the weakness of human knowledge. This befits the roseate view of Sophocles as a pious, highly religious man, but as a character in E. M. Forster's *The Longest Journey* remarks – 'Boys will regard Sophocles as a kind of enlightened bishop, and something tells me that they are wrong'[9] – there may be more to say on this matter. Does it necessarily follow from the Delphic oracle proving to be correct that Jocasta's view of life as ontologically open, without design, is therefore mistaken? If so, then this would seem to diminish man's freedom; if Oedipus was a victim of fate, his course through life already known, the value of knowledge seems pitifully limited. We are reduced to knowledge of the phenomenal world only and must remain at the mercy of larger forces directing and designing our lives. It is dangerous to think our human understanding can rival the metaphysical knowledge that belongs only to the gods and those few prophets who are entrusted with the ability to pass on some inkling of it. In this case, Oedipus' mistake was to think otherwise, boasting to Teiresias:

> But I came,
> Oedipus, who knew nothing, and I stopped her [the Sphinx].
> I solved the riddle by my wit alone.
> Mine was no knowledge got from birds.

> (396–398)

In what could be a play on his name, Oedipus 'knew nothing' (*mēden eidōs Oidipous*) because by foolishly prioritizing rational intelligence he discredited and failed to acknowledge another level of understanding and this undermines his claim to possess knowledge. It has been observed how for much of the play Oedipus is the constant questioner but when he does arrive at the final answer and understanding dawns, it is too late:[10] 'The owl of Minerva spreads its wings only with the falling of dusk'; referring to Athena (the Roman Minerva), the goddess of wisdom and patron of Athens, Hegel's metaphor can be aligned with an awareness that only comes to Oedipus after the event, after the happenings of the day.[11] As the chorus exclaims (1200ff.), the knowledge that he drove himself to establish has cast a retrospective unhappiness over the entire course of his life; 'Sophocles dramatizes a crisis in which humans try, and fail, to write their own stories.'[12] Fate, it seems, decreed that he would kill his father and become husband to his own mother but it was Oedipus' own choice to relentlessly pursue an investigation into the circumstances of Laius' death. His own choice? The oracle that Creon consulted on behalf of Oedipus said that the plague afflicting Thebes would be lifted if the death of Laius was avenged and this can be seen as another arm of fate directing Oedipus to investigate and identify himself as the cause of the problem.

Fate

In *Paradise Lost* (ii.558–561) Milton describes how the more intellectually inclined of the fallen angels retired to a hill and:

> reason'd high
> Of Providence, Foreknowledge, Will, and Fate,
> Fixt Fate, Free will, Foreknowledge absolute,
> And found no end, in wand'ring mazes lost.[13]

It is not surprising the angels find themselves lost in 'wand'ring mazes' given the antinomies and paradoxes that abound in their chosen topics for discussion. Fate can be pictured as a strange combination of accident and implacable necessity and the uncanny emergence of truth from misapprehension, as in the story about an appointment in Samara as told by Somerset Maugham in his play *Sheppey*:

> There was a merchant in Baghdad who sent his servant to market to buy provisions and in a little while the servant came back, white and trembling, and said, Master, just now when I was in the marketplace I was jostled by a woman in the crowd and when I turned I saw it was Death that jostled me. She looked at me and made a threatening gesture; now, lend me your horse, and I will ride away from this city and avoid my fate. I will go to Samarra and there Death will not find me. The merchant lent him his horse, and the servant mounted it, and he dug his spurs in its flanks and as fast as the horse could gallop he went. Then the merchant went down to the market-place and he saw me standing in the crowd and he came to me and said, Why did you make a threatening gesture to my servant when you saw him this morning? That was not a threatening gesture, I said, it was only a start of surprise. I was astonished to see him in Baghdad, for I had an appointment with him tonight in Samarra.[14]

The servant who flees to Samara is the victim of a fate which is as singular as it is stringent for everything that happens possesses an inherent inevitability, it seems, and the links in the causal chain are adamantine. Contingency seems outlawed and yet, as in *Oedipus*, accident is at the heart of events.

Another way of approaching the temporal paradox at the heart of discussions about fate and freedom is the sci-fi plot line where someone travels into the past in order to change the present only to subsequently realize that the present he sought to change was brought about *because* of his intervention. What this illustrates is how time seems to follow a linear 'objective' projecture, but actually contains within it subjective loops that help account for what happened.[15] The course of Oedipus' life, after the event, can be reinscribed into the 'straight line' of historical time, but it was unprescribed, dependent on his subjective engagement at certain crucial moments. Or was it? Talk of fate can also tap into a sense of the uncanny, which can be expressed portentously – as in Iris Murdoch:

> One perceives a subterranean current, one feels the grip of destiny, striking coincidences do occur and the world is full of signs: such things are not necessarily senseless or symptoms of incipient paranoia. They can indeed be the shadows of a real not yet apprehended metamorphosis. Coming events do leave shadows.[16]

– comically as in Samuel Beckett's *Watt*:

> And if I could begin it all over again, knowing what I know now, the result would be the same. And if I could begin again, a third time, knowing what I would know then, the result would be the same. And if I could begin it all over again a hundred times, knowing each time a little more than the time before, the result would always be the same, and the hundredth life as the first, and the hundred lives as one. A cat's flux. But at this rate we shall be here all night.[17]

– or with the baffled curiosity found in J. G. Ballard's *Millennium People* when Sally Markham, injured in a railway accident, continues to occasionally use a wheelchair, refusing to admit her physical recovery from the accident:

> It was her curious obsession with the random nature of the accident that prevented her from walking . . . 'I'm waiting for an answer . . . It's the most important question there is.'
> 'Go on.'
> '"Why me?" Answer it. You can't.'
> 'Sally . . . does it matter? It's a fluke we're alive at all. The chance of our parents meeting were millions to one against. We're tickets in a lottery.'
> 'But a lottery isn't meaningless. Someone has to win.'[18]

Ancient Greece looked at issues of fate and chance in its own ways – through myths, tragic drama and more particularly oracles – and these forms of thinking combine in a fairly unique way in *Oedipus*. On one level of reading, the play seems to outlaw contingency given that three different prophecies (four if Teiresias' prediction of what will happen to Oedipus is included) all correctly foresee a certain outcome. When Oedipus is arguing with Teiresias and dismisses his riddling taunts as the utterances of a senile and senseless man, the prophet points to the source of his mantic power:

> It is not fate that I should be your ruin,
> Apollo is enough; it is his care
> to work this out.

> (376–377)

This is close to being a literal translation of the Greek and it points to a curse on Oedipus that existed before he was born and which the god Apollo will ensure runs its proper course. The links in the causal chains that lead to the Delphic oracles being fulfilled seem inflexible and yet accident is at the heart of the drama for there are any number of moments where a chance event could have led to a different outcome. If Oedipus had arrived at the crossroads half an hour later there would have been no 'road rage' incident or if Jocasta had omitted the detail that Laius was killed where three roads meet, all might have been different. What would have been the outcome if the messenger from Corinth had not arrived to inform Oedipus of the rumour that he might become the new king of Thebes? Chance (*tukhē*), says Oedipus, is what leaped upon Laius (262) and the same word is used by Teiresias: 'It is this very luck (*tukhē*) that has destroyed you' (442).[19] Most European words for 'happy' originally meant lucky, as in English where the word comes from a root *happ* meaning chance, and Oedipus' happiness can be seen as being destroyed by chance events over which he had no control. Jocasta, just before she returns to the palace for the last time having failed to persuade Oedipus to cease his inquiries, calls him 'unhappy' (*dustēne*) for 'this is all I can call you, and the last thing that I shall ever call you' (1071–1072).

Different possibilities always exist and the ones that happen to unfold lead to particular punctual moments regardless of the degree of premeditation – Oedipus did not plan to arrive at the crossroads at the same time as Laius – but in order to account for what happened in a rational way events can be retroactively positioned so as to produce a causal chain that makes the result appear inevitable. The event, the effect of something contingent, can be accounted for by positing necessity as its cause. This occludes the contingency at the heart of the matter and allows necessity to be presented as an organizing force. If so, the force of necessity is retrospective and the inevitability it imposes comes about because of an intrinsically accidental event or events; something that is perhaps there in the background when we speak of 'a simple twist of fate', the inexplicable moment that determines that which follows and in a way that could never be foreseen (unless you are Apollo). Simple twists of fate combine to dictate that Jocasta's unwanted son returns to his homeland as her husband and a parricide and what engages the attention of the audience is seeing how a series of accidental events turn into a pattern of necessity. Such a sense of necessity – which could be called fate – is not contradicted by ideas of selfhood and a freedom of the will; necessity need not be implacable but just the name for the outcome of our actions. In this sense, we push our own wheel of necessity and as it turns we assume our fate.

While a chain of causal necessity implies an ontologically consistent world, the utter contingency that can determine a significant moment, the infinite possibilities that could result in such a moment never coming into existence, points to a world that is ontologically incoherent. Jocasta looks to this inconsistency, the lack of any pattern, as a source of comfort and accepts the subjunctive as a part of reality's grammar. She tells Oedipus, worried about returning to Corinth after the death of his supposed father in case the other half of the prophecy, concerning sex with his mother, were to be fulfilled: 'Why should man fear since chance is all in all / for him, and he can clearly foreknow nothing?' (977–978).

For the philosopher Žižek there is another kind of comfort to be found in such a meaningless universe, the kind that allows Oedipus to gain the autonomy that drives him to seek out the truth:

> the only way really to account for the status of freedom is to assert *the ontological incompleteness of 'reality' itself*: there is 'reality' only in so far as there is an ontological gap, a crack, at its very heart. It is only this gap which accounts for the mysterious 'fact' of transcendental freedom – for the 'self-positing' subjectivity which is in fact 'spontaneous', whose spontaneity is not an effect of misrecognition of some 'objective' causal process, no matter how complex and chaotic this process is.[20]

As he approaches the scene of recognition, just before the herdsman appears, Oedipus accepts the 'ontological incompleteness' of life and accounts for himself as a child of Chance (*paida tēs Tukhēs*, 1080), concurring with Jocasta at the very moment that he chooses to ignore her advice and confront what Chance has brought him.

This antinomy between the necessity of fate and the freedom of a reality based on contingency is something that Oedipus gives voice to when he finds himself in the grip of contradictory forces and, appearing to the chorus after blinding himself, states:

> It was Apollo, friends, Apollo,
> that brought this bitter bitterness, my sorrow to completion.
> But the hand that struck me
> was none but my own.
>
> (1329–1332)

He regards his self-blinding as the autonomous act of an individual self as if in contrast to, or complementing, the controlling force of a god whose force he acknowledges but not to the exclusion of his own will. However, the prophet Teiresias knew Oedipus would lose his sight (454), predicting his 'blindness for sight' (*tuphlos gar ek dedorkotos*), so even his act of self-blinding can be viewed as another element in an overall design. Such a design, if there is one, could be as binding as that of predestination or as loose as that of an emerging pattern that was never designed as such but nonetheless has an arrangement that lifts it above the chaotic. In this way, Oedipus 'can look back on his previously benighted self and recognize that his life forms an intelligible whole, however devoutly he may wish that it did not'.[21]

The first mention of an oracle in the play is when Creon returns from Delphi and reports that the oracle there (the actual words are never given) attributes the city's plague to the killing of the former king and states that the pollution this caused can only be expiated by banishing or putting to death those responsible. When Oedipus is told he is the killer by Teiresias, Jocasta tries to put his mind at rest by showing how an oracle was disproved. She tells how an oracle came to her first husband Laius and it said it was fate that he should die at the hands of his own child (*hōs auton hexoi moira pros paidos thenein*, 713). The word she uses that is translated as fate is *moira* (as in 376–377 above), a term meaning one's portion in life, one's lot or destiny. Later, after the herdsman who witnessed the slaying of Laius has been summoned to give his evidence and hopefully rule out the likelihood that Oedipus was the killer, the chorus begins their third ode by praying that their *moira* keeps them safe (863–865) and that a bad *moira* will afflict those who misbehave (882–891).[22]

The heavy weight of fate that seems to hang over Oedipus, robbing his life of value and destroying everything that gave him a sense of autonomy and self-belief, suggests a doom-laden, pagan belief that, no matter what, we cannot escape the consequences of our past acts. We do not know it, but they follow like ghostly footsteps and sooner or later catch up with us and demand that the debt be settled. In the myth of Oedipus, the 'debt' goes back to when his father Laius was staying in the house of Pisa with Pelops, a time before he was able to claim his legitimate right to rule Thebes. Laius fell in love with a son of Pelops, Chrysippus, kidnapped him and took him to Thebes to make him his catamite. But Chrysippus was so ashamed that he committed suicide and in his grief Pelops laid a curse on Laius. Zeus, hearing of the curse, pronounced that as a punishment Laius would be killed by his own son.[23]

The story of the curse on Laius is not referred to in *Oedipus* but some knowledge of it is implied by the fact that the oracle Jocasta tells Oedipus about, prophesying that Laius would be killed by his offspring, reached her husband in Thebes before she had given birth to their son (711–714). Oedipus is cursed before he is born, fated to kill his father before he is even formed in the womb of his mother. If this is part of the play's tragic vision, it is a particularly stifling aspect that closes down on life's possibilities by fusing the ontological – our existence in this world – with ethical questions about how we should live. We are guilty because we exist, an inescapable trap that was closed before we were born, and as the chorus' last words state: 'Count no mortal happy till he has passed the final limit of his life secure from pain' (1529–1530). Žižek has noted how this grim mentality is captured in the Greek word *aitia*, which carries both the sense of a cause, a reason, and that of culpability, responsibility and guilt,[24] and it finds an echo in Oedipus' self-reflexive question in response to Creon's account of Apollo's command that the murderer of Laius be punished:

Where would a trace
of this old crime [*aitia*] be found?

(108–109)

The sense of fate like the theme of knowledge in *Oedipus* is bound up with philosophical issues, this time to do with freewill and necessity. There are two prophecies issuing from Delphi that predict what turns out to be the case, one reaching Laius before his son is born and one told to Oedipus as a young man; the Delphic oracle also gives information to Creon about the cause of the plague in Thebes which sets off an investigation by Oedipus and leads him to discovering that the earlier two prophecies were true. One can add Teiresias, who as a prophet can be seen as a messenger of Apollo, and count four divine interventions that create the sense of certainty that Oedipus could not escape his destiny. It had been mapped out for him and, regardless of what he thinks he is doing, he has no choice but to follow its course. And Oedipus does try to escape such a destiny when, hearing the prophecy about his own dire future, he fled from Corinth and thus found himself at a road junction when Laius happened to be passing, a circumstance that led to the first part of the prophecy being fulfilled. Or, to go further back, it was the attempt by Laius to avoid the prophecy he had heard saying he would be killed by his son (a son not born at the time) that led to Oedipus being abandoned on the mountain side and so ending up in Corinth in the first place. The coincidences appear to be too uncanny to be just coincidences; Oedipus cannot escape what is going to happen and, like the man from Samara, if he tries to, then the noose only tightens.

But at the same time, the outcome that seems inevitable is brought about as the result of his individual qualities of mind. It is his will and determination to establish the truth of his own identity that brings matters to their unwanted conclusion. Surely we are one with an Athenian audience in feeling that the man who replies to the herdsman's warning of 'I am on the brink of frightful speech' . . . with 'And I of frightful hearing. But I must hear' (1069–1070) is not being manipulated by the gods into displaying the courage to pursue the truth at whatever the cost. The prophecies predict what will take place, not that Oedipus will come to know their truth *because of* his strength of mind, his force of will. But then again, even here, there are bizarre coincidences that ensure the success of Oedipus' quest: the survivor of the altercation at the crossroads is the same man who out of pity saved the life of the infant Oedipus, giving him to a Corinthian who happens to be the same man who comes to Thebes with news of the death of Polybus and who just happens to arrive in Thebes at the very moment when the killing of Laius is being investigated.

Contingency and necessity follow each other in a circle unless the opposition between the two terms can be seen as allowing for a narrative to be produced which transforms the contingent into the necessary. What remains open, following a rationale put forward by Žižek, is a choice of how we symbolize and make sense of what happens – fate, destiny, an arbitrary causal chain, chaos theory, an ideology, are some of the possibilities – and this choice is itself contingent. What happens is open to us to symbolize: 'freedom is . . . the (contingent) choice of the modality by means of which we symbolize the contingent real or impose some narrative necessity upon it'.[25] Such a confluence of necessity and contingency illustrates the movement of the Hegelian dialectic, though not in the traditional and simplistic way whereby the synthesis of the two terms (the overused and misleading dichotomy of thesis and antithesis) are simply reduced to and subordinated within a moment of sublation (*Aufhebung*), preserving contingency in some larger, overall moment of necessity. Instead, the split between chance and necessity is reflected back into the identity of whatever mode we choose to homogenize and make sense of what has taken place. If, to choose just one of the moments that have important consequences, a drunk had not accused Oedipus of being illegitimate (780–788), then there would have been no visit to Delphi to try and ascertain the truth of the accusation, no fleeing from Corinth, no meeting at the crossroads and so on. The whole of the rest of Oedipus' life would have been different and, if we look to fate as our narrative mode, the 'necessity' governing his life would have an altered shape. Fate, as John Lennon might have said, is what happens to us when we're busy making other plans.

Oedipus' feet

References to feet occur in ancient Greek texts with a regularity that seems eccentrically disproportionate to modern sensibilities and in this play, given the name of its eponymous hero, the topic takes on a peculiar resonance. One possible etymology for the word *oidipous* – referring to 'knowing' – has already been mentioned but the word could also come from *oideō* 'to swell' and *pous* the Greek for 'foot' (thus Shelley's *Swellfoot the Tyrant* as his title for a satirical play he wrote in 1820), and the idea that Oedipus' identity is bound up with his bound feet is referred to by the messenger from Corinth when it turns out that it was he who was given the infant by the herdsman working for Laius.

> I loosed you;
> the tendons of your feet were pierced and fettered . . .
> So that from this you're called your present name.
>
> (1034, 1036)

When the two possible etymologies are conjoined something like 'the knower of feet' comes out and this possesses its own peculiar quality as a name for Oedipus in view of the fact that his knowledgeable awareness of feet is what allows him to solve the Sphinx's riddle (not actually recited in the play) – what walks on four feet in the morning, two in the afternoon but three in the evening? Oedipus not only solved the Sphinx's poser about feet but he comes to embody it in the course of his life. He becomes the answer to the riddle: the helpless infant who crawls on feet and hands after his pinned ankles are unbound, the upright adult who stood on his own two feet when challenged by a stranger, finally and prematurely the three-footed man at the play's end who needs the aid of a stick in order to find his way.

There are a number of references to feet in *Oedipus* but maybe they amount to more of an enigma about the way feet are metaphorized in ancient Greek literature than to a conscious design on the part of the playwright. Sometimes, as at line 130 where Creon speaks of 'troubles at our feet' he may be only speaking figuratively, referring to 'matters of immediate unease', and attempts to incorporate such a remark into a putative theme could be the result of an over-zealous search for signs.[26] On the other hand, Creon is referring to how the 'riddling Sphinx' (*hē poikilōdos Sphigx*) was preoccupying the city and a reference to feet at this moment does carry a certain resonance even if unintended. At line 479 the Chorus is describing the plight of the murderer of Laius, fleeing and hiding – 'sad and lonely, and lonely his feet' (*meleos meleō podi khēreuōn*) – but again the expression may have more to do with the vernacular than the symbolic. Notwithstanding, for the critic Vernant the feet of Oedipus are a key to the drama:

Pous: 'the foot'– the mark imposed since birth on him whose destiny is to finish as he began, excluded, like the savage beast which his *foot* makes flee (468), whom his *foot* isolates from humans, in the vain hope of escaping the oracles (479 ff.), pursued by the curse with the terrible *foot* (417) for having transgressed the sacred laws with his lifted foot (866), and incapable from then on of extricating his foot from the evils into which he has precipitated himself by raising himself to the height of power. The whole tragedy of Oedipus is thus contained in the play to which the riddle of his name lends itself. To that wise, knowing master of Thebes, whom happy omen protects, is at every point opposed the cursed infant, the Swollen Foot cast out of his fatherland.[27]

For the ancient Greeks it is not just feet that attract what to us sometimes seems like an odd degree of attention. When Oedipus greets his wife, after she has summoned him to hear news of Polybus' death in Corinth, he addresses her with affection as his 'dearest wife' (950), literally 'O dearest head of my wife Jocasta' (*ō philaton gunaikos Iokastēs kara*) and when the messenger reports the death of Jocasta (1235) he announces, literally, 'the divine head of Jocasta has died' (*tethnēke theion Iokastēs kara*).

Notes

1 Williams (1994), p. 69.

2 Unlike *The Phoenician Women* by Euripides, set after the events of *Oedipus*, where Antigone scolds her father for boasting of his success in defeating the Sphinx.

3 Quoted in Regier (2004), p. 3.

4 Kant (2007), p. 41 (B1).

5 Ibid., p. 126 (B126).

6 Jones (1980), p. 168.

7 Goldhill (1986), p. 220.

8 Burian (1992), pp. 199–201.

9 E. M. Forster (1992), p. 161.

10 'The characteristic tone of Oedipus in the first two thirds of the play is that of an impatient, demanding questioner'. Knox (1957), p. 121.

11 Hegel (1975), p. 13.

12 Bushnell (1988), pp. 84–85.

13 Milton (1962), p. 44.

14 http://en.wikipedia.org/wiki/Sheppey_%28play%29

15 Žižek (2003), pp. 134–135.

16 Murdoch (1973), p.113.

17 Beckett (1976), p. 46.

18 Ballard (2004), pp. 24–25.

19 Indeed, the word *tukhē* (lines 52, 80, 102, 263, 442, 680, 776, 997, 1036, 1080) occurs far more often in the play than *moira*.

20 Žižek (2002), pp. 174–175.

21 Eagleton (2003), p. 42.

22 'Although appearing relatively rarely throughout the play, *moira* presents a certain conceptual stability. In its first and last occurrence, by Teiresias and by the chorus, respectively, it seems to be used to represent the personal *moira* of Oedipus. In between, it appears as a more active character, something of an enforcer – holding someone to fulfil a future action, finding someone out, punishing the haughty for breaking cosmic laws of order.' Eidinow (2011), pp. 56–57.

23 For a full account of the various myths surrounding Thebes, founded by Cadmus, the great-grandfather of Laius, see March (2009), pp. 264–293.

24 Žižek (2002), p. 53.

25 Žižek (2005), p. 36.

26 A point of view astringently expressed by one editor: 'the tasteless possibility has presented itself to some minds that there is here some allusion to the "foot" enigma'. Dawe (2006), p. 84.

27 Vernant (1983), p. 197.

CHAPTER FOUR

Reading *Oedipus*

Suppliants petition Oedipus (1–86)

The drama begins with a public scene outside the king's palace in Thebes where a group of citizens have gathered, with an elderly priest of the city as their spokesperson. In the surviving Greek tragedies it is very uncommon for the protagonist to be the object of supplication and this can be taken as an indication of the unusual state of affair – there is something rotten in the state of Thebes – that occasions this play's opening.

As suppliants the citizens carry branches of olive or laurel garlanded with wool; in another part of the city, we learn in line 20, other citizens sit with their wreathed branches by two temples of Pallas Athena and at a shrine to Apollo where burnt offerings were read by priests as oracular pronouncements. This opening scene, then, laden with ritualistic overtones, shows a community of the Theban *polis* appealing to both the secular and the divine, desperately seeking help in the face of a virulent plague. Trauma is a Greek word meaning an external injury, a wound, and it is in this tangible sense that the plight of the *polis* is rendered: heard in hymns of lamentation, smelt in the burning incense, seen in the blight-infected cattle and fruit, in the failure of women to give normal birth. With death all around, striking indiscriminately and for an unknown reason, the modern sense of an injury to the mind can also be sensed; the Theban community is traumatized.

There is a certain irony in the way Oedipus introduces himself in line 8 – 'I Oedipus renowned of all' (*ho pasi kleinos Oidipous*) in Jebb's translation – given that for an audience, Greek or modern, the source of his renown lies in what the course of the play is about to reveal, in what he will come to know about himself. The immediate matter, though, is the state of his *polis* and his feeling of solicitation, a sentiment he reiterates (60–64) before explaining that he has already taken some action that hopefully will lead to a remedy. His proven success in dealing with the capriciousness of life, the priest explains, is what distinguishes him and motivates their arrival as suppliants:

> [not] because we thought of you as a God,
> but rather judging you the first of men
> in all the chances of this life

> (32–34)

The priest is careful to make a distinction between the power of the gods and that of mortals. Oedipus, in solving the riddle of the Sphinx, has shown himself master of the rational but, as the priest adds immediately to the lines just quoted, his success owes something to that inscrutable dimension that lies beyond our ken 'it was God that aided you, men say, and you are held with God's assistance to have saved our lives'.

The irony here is double layered. At one level, given our knowledge of what has happened and what is yet to come, the audience knows that the chances of life (*sumphorais biou*) have prepared a nasty surprise for Oedipus. This is what makes the irony deeper: he is 'the first of men' in a way the priest could never have intended, as an exemplar of tragic misfortune, of what can befall anyone if chance works against them. Whether Oedipus' past action is associated with the numinous or the result of arbitrary chance, this is a world where intentions will be out of kilter with events. This is what lies behind *peripeteia*, a reversal in fortune that is always possible because it springs from the profound indeterminacy at the heart of everything and, since this indeterminacy goes to the heart of human existence, Oedipus is indeed exemplary. He is the 'first of men' or, as Hölderlin translated this line, 'the first in happenings/ of the world'.[1]

A remorseless shadow of irony is cast over everything Oedipus says in this scene:

> . . . I know you are all sick
> yet there is not one of you, sick though you are,

that is sick as I myself.

(59–61)

He identifies the city's suffering with his own, though not in the way that will soon become apparent. When he speaks of 'the many roads of thought' that he travelled to find a cure for the city, the audience may think of the non-metaphorical roads he travelled which brought him to Thebes and the crossroads where he killed his father. This killing is about to be revealed as the source of the sickness that presently afflicts the city.

Creon's approach is heralded and Oedipus expresses the hope that he brings good fortune. The simile he uses, literally translated as 'like a bright eye' (81), links to the images of sight and blindness, light and dark – and, metaphorically, knowledge and ignorance – that will haunt the language of the drama.

Creon returns from the oracle at Delphi (87–150)

Oracles and the notion of pollution are two aspects of ancient Greek culture that make their presence felt in this scene but which, being both very familiar to the intended audience, they do not arouse dramatic force until specific details are announced by Creon: the plague is due to the killing of Laius, the former king, and the consequent pollution can only be expiated by banishing or putting to death the killer. Oedipus, in his role as carer of the community, insists that the oracle be made public and in the first of his forensic-style investigations, he asks a series of pointed questions – who, where, what, how? – in an attempt to find some trace, some cause, of the crime. The word *ichnos* (109) that is translated as 'trace' or 'track' can also mean footprint or an animal's spoor, a mark which can be followed, and this links to the play's foot imagery and the hunting trope that runs through the drama. But when Creon says 'they were all killed save one. He fled in terror' (118), Oedipus does not follow this 'footstep' pointing to the one vital witness at the scene of the crime and focuses instead on Creon's 'one thing' – Laius was killed by a group of killers.[2] Also, in what might be seen as literature's inaugural Freudian slip, Oedipus seems to ignore this information about there being a group of murderers (122) and, instead, uses the singular in the very next line. It will be some six hundred lines later that the importance of this sole witness resurfaces (754–755).

Oedipus respects Apollo's solicitude for an unresolved act of homicide and publicly announces that he wants to take on the responsibility for justly carrying out the god's mandate: 'you will see in me an ally (*summakhon*)', he proclaims, 'a champion of my country and the God'(135–136). He adds that whoever killed one king is capable of making an attempt on the life of another ruler, like himself, so self-interest strengthens his resolve to find the unknown assassin.

His preliminary investigation over, the scene comes to a conclusion with an announcement of intent: he will start afresh, from the beginning (*ex huparkhesi*), and as with the verb he confidently employs in this line (132) 'I will bring to light' (*phano*), his choice of words is troublingly portentous: returning to the beginning will render visible what until now has remained buried in the dark, according it a potency that will rewrite the history of Thebes, Oedipus and his family.

Oedipus proceeds in a highly rational way: putting eleven questions to Creon in forty lines (89–129) soliciting essential information, deducing the probability that the killer of Laius would have had financial backers in Thebes, thus the possibility of a political assassination, before concluding that his own life as ruler may be in danger. He reassures the suppliants and calls an assembly. This is a competent and caring king, the kind of man whose lucid rationality was able to deal successfully with the Sphinx and who now fully expects to be able to deal with the crisis that has so affected his city.

The parode (151–215)

The prologue at an end, the chorus enters the empty *orchestra* from each of the two corridors to its side and sings its first ode. The words of this choral ode have a solemnity that comes not just from what is being said but from the formal, choreographed mode of expression: sung to music and accompanied by dance-like movements as the chorus moves across the *orchestra*. The chorus provides a ritual quality to Athenian drama that goes back to its possible origins in rites celebrating Dionysus, and this is intensified in the first ode in *Oedipus* by it being an address to the gods by a group of Theban elders. Its purpose is apotropaic, designed to avert evil, but the first strophe transcends the rhetorical aspect of this because of the audience's awareness that the chorus has good reason to fear what lies behind the 'sweet-sounding' (*haduepes*) message coming jointly from Zeus and his son the 'Delian Healer' (Apollo) in 'Pytho' (Delphi).

The antistrophe calls on Athena, Artemis and Apollo (Phoebus and Far Shooter are two of Apollo's epithets) to 'come to us now', (*prophanete* in line 165 comes from *phano*, more literally meaning 'to show light'). The lamentations of the second strophe and antistrophe are followed by more invocations: Ares, the god of war, becomes a personification of the plague and the cry is for Zeus to banish him to the 'palace of Amphitrite' (wife of Poseidon, god of the sea) or the Thracian coast (far away in northern Greece). The arrows of Apollo (the 'Lycean King'), the burning torches of Artemis, the god Bacchus and his female followers, the Maenads, are all called upon to rid Thebes of the unhonoured, pestilent god of war.

The play's first ode is as passionate as it is liturgical and if it is true that the plague that devastated Athens early on in the Peloponnesian War, as documented by Thucydides, is the felt context for the pestilence afflicting Thebes, then this may help explain the heightened, desperate nature of the appeal by the chorus. (It might also help account for the god of war being blamed for the devastation, see page 7.) There is a Homeric quality to many of the epithets employed by the chorus – 'deathless daughter of Zeus . . . Earth Upholder . . . Far Shooter' – as if the Theban elders are driven to evoke ancient, demonical forces and far-flung places beyond the pale (the 'palace of Amphitrite' probably refers to the Atlantic) in order to express their existential fear in the face of the plague.

Oedipus responds to the chorus (216–315)

Oedipus responds to the prayers of the elders by first explaining that he is proceeding in a certain way because at the time Laius was

killed he was not in Thebes and was therefore unable to conduct a
proper inquest. Now, though, despite the passage of time he will
set about the task and he begins with an announcement:

> Hark to me; what I say to you, I say
> as one that is a stranger [*xenos*] to the story
> as stranger to the deed.
>
> (218–220)

The irony doubles back on itself: unlike the speaker, the audience
knows that what is being said is not true, but that the man who
killed Laius, although his son, was a stranger to him and he was
also *xenos*, as someone coming from the outside towards Thebes
when he encountered the men at the crossroads.

The oracle says that responsibility for the killing of Laius can be
found in Thebes (110) and Oedipus proceeds to issue a proclamation calling upon any citizen with information to come forward.
No one need fear for their life even if they incriminate themselves.
If someone responsible is not prepared to come forward, or if someone is withholding vital evidence, Oedipus formally banishes him
from Thebes and he issues a religious excommunication by forbid-
ding his participation in the ritual of sacrifice.[3] The murderer is
cursed and Oedipus declares his intent to find whoever was responsible for the death of Laius, an act of self-condemnation that comes
about because of his piety and the sincerity he brings to carrying
out the god's wishes. The strength of feeling and the solemnity that
Oedipus invests in his curse on the unknown killer is given its full
weight in the translation by Berg and Clay; it is a translation more
poetic than literal in its handling of the Greek *ektripsai bion* (to
rub out his life):

> My words are his doom.
> Whether he did it alone, and escaped unseen,
> whether others helped him kill, it makes no difference –
> let my hatred burn out his life, hatred, always.
> Make him an ember of suffering.
> Make all his happiness
> ashes.
>
> (246–249)

Oedipus' address to the chorus is grimly layered with irony. There is little spoken that does not carry another meaning for the audience and in places this could hardly be more explicit:

> If with my knowledge he lives at my hearth
> I pray that I myself may feel my curse

> (250–251)

In lines 220–221, the irony is more subtle. Had he not been a stranger to the events surrounding the killing of Laius, he reasons, had he been in Thebes when the event happened, he would not have needed an exhaustive search to find a clue. He is as unaware of the untruth of this first remark – he is no stranger to the events – as he is of the truth that a clue was close at hand. The word translated as clue, *sumbolon* (giving us the word 'symbol'), has the sense of a token of identity, a tally. Athenian jurors were given a *sumbolon* when attending a court case, a token which could be exchanged for another one which entitled them to be paid for their attendance. When this sense of *sumbolon* is brought into play, Oedipus' remark becomes ironically self-reflexive for we realize that he is his own clue and it is himself he would have been looking for; the clue he would have needed could not have been closer.

The irony takes a hideous tack when Oedipus explains why his obligation to find the killer rests so heavily upon his shoulders (260–262). He has replaced Laius as both king and husband (this is the first reference to Oedipus' marriage, although Jocasta is not mentioned by name) and has had children with the woman who was once the man's wife. Had Laius and his wife had offspring of their own, reasons Oedipus, the child or children would be kin to the children born afterwards to himself and Laius' widow. The ghastly double-meanings at work here point to the incest of Oedipus with his mother and the incestuous consequences: Laius and his wife did have a child (Oedipus) and this child is indeed kin (father and brother) to the children born later to Laius' widow and Oedipus.

Laius, says Oedipus, was unlucky (*dustukhesēn*) because, in Grene's literal translation of the phrase that follows, '[ill]fortune leaped upon his head' (262) with his untimely death in a childless state. Laius was unfortunate, but not childless and chance (*tukhē*) proved truly appalling when it also leaped on Oedipus' head and took the form it did.

Oedipus' vow to trace the murderer is expressed in grand, historic terms as he traces Laius' lineage (266–268) back through time to beyond the founder of Thebes, Cadmus (himself instructed by a Delphic oracle to establish a city by sowing the teeth of a dragon), unwittingly tracing his own history, unaware he has extended the family line to another generation.

The play of double meanings continues in the response to Oedipus' proclamation by the chorus leader and a note of ironic doom accompanies its dialogue welcoming the arrival of one in whom the truth is implanted (*talēthes empephuken*).

Oedipus and Teiresias (297–462)

This agon, an argumentative debate between opponents, starts with the arrival of the seer and his silent presence as Oedipus addresses him with a request for information Teiresias possesses but does not wish to impart; it ends, in reverse, with the seer addressing a mute Oedipus who hears the information he had requested but remains unable to understand its import.

Oedipus initially treats Teiresias with great respect and is puzzled by his request to be allowed to return home. Three more attempts are made by Oedipus to solicit from him some constructive information before his exasperation breaks out. Yet Teiresias still refuses to reveal anything and, after he adamantly declares that he never will, Oedipus finally loses his temper and accuses the prophet of being involved in the plot to murder Laius. Teiresias is now provoked into breaking his resolve to say nothing and he states that Oedipus himself is the polluter of the land. Oedipus angrily dismisses the prophet, adding (430) 'and a curse go with you' (*ouk eis olethron*).

It is hard to find solid evidence in this exchange for some tragic flaw in Oedipus' makeup that inclines him towards violence. Both men prove to be irascible and it is Oedipus' determination to find the killer of Laius and thereby save the city from further grief that fuels his growing anger at Teiresias' withholding of information.

One man's resolve to seek knowledge of the killing is matched by the other man's desire to hide it and the clash of wills results in both of them saying more than they ever intended at the start of their conversation.

Questions surrounding the nature of knowledge, which are allied here to issues of seeing and not seeing, dominate this scene from the very start. Teiresias is hailed by Oedipus in one line (300) as 'observing mentally' (*nōmōn*) both what can be taught and what cannot be spoken. This introduces a distinction between the knowledge of experiential reality and another more intangible order of knowledge. A paradoxical instance of the latter is Teiresias' awareness (316–317) that sometimes it is better not to know when what is known brings in its wake cognizance of something terrible. This is not just the resigned conservatism of one who prefers the status quo to the threat of something new: what Teiresias knows (341) is that Oedipus will come to know his own history and regret possessing such knowledge and there is nothing he, Teiresias, can do to stop this (*hēxei gar auta*). It is the refusal to acknowledge the logical force of Oedipus' reply – if it will happen anyway then why not say so now – that provokes the accusation that Teiresias was involved in the conspiracy to kill Laius.

In line 376 Teiresias asserts that he is not to blame for what will befall Oedipus and links *moira* (fate) with Apollo. Oedipus has no time for this, regarding it as part of a subterfuge involving Creon, and vindicates his reasoning by discrediting the worth of omens. What use was the power of interpreting omens, he argues, when the Sphinx posed her deadly riddle?

> I solved the riddle by my wit alone
> Mine was no knowledge got from birds.

> (398–399)

His 'wit' is *gnōmē*, the rational intelligence that he is now applying to the mystery of Laius' murder. The response of Teiresias is a demonstration of another kind of intelligence, his foreknowledge of what is to come:

> blindness for sight
> and beggary for riches his exchange,

he shall go journeying to a foreign country
tapping his way before him with a stick.

(454–456)

Oedipus' perception of the truth will make him blind and reliant
on the aid of a stick, departing the city as one of the figures of
human life referred to in the riddle of the Sphinx. This will come
about because he will find the answer to Teiresias' stark, query
about his origins (415). 'Do you know from who you are?' is the
question posed in monosyllabic Greek (*ar' oisth' aph' hōn ei*) and
Teiresias immediately adds that his ignorance of this has made
him an enemy to his own kin. He concludes his frightening prophecy of what will befall Oedipus with a forbiddingly dark two-line
summary –

No man will ever know worse suffering than you,
your life, your flesh, your happiness an ember of pain. Ashes.

(427–428, Berg and Clay)

– using the same verb of annihilation (*ektribēsetai*), meaning 'to
rub out', that Oedipus used when issuing his curse just a short
while earlier (246–249).

Teiresias is prophesying the painful truth that Oedipus will come
to experience in all its horror and, in the line-by-line dialogue (*stichomythia*) that follows, Oedipus himself asks the same question
about the identity of his parents (437). He does not at this moment
dwell further on the thought, but, as with the remaining lines of
this dialogue, there is a pregnant meaning in the words spoken.
Oedipus finds the prophet's remarks riddling and Teiresias, thinking of the boast made earlier about the Sphinx's riddle, reminds
him that puzzles are what he should be good at solving. Oedipus
thinks this is a cheap jibe:

Oedipus: Yes. Taunt me where you will find me great.
Teiresias: It is this very luck that has destroyed you.

(441–442)

Oedipus' skill, his claim to fame, was demonstrated by his success with the Sphinx and this rational intelligence is what he intends to apply in order to deal with the plight of Thebes. Undermining this is Teiresias' statement that what seems to have brought him success is not human knowledge, but the result of chance (*tukhē*) and it is chance that has destroyed his life. At this stage of events, such remarks can only strike Oedipus as riddles of another kind and the tragedy is that he will soon solve these riddles, those concerning his own identity, and then his sense of successful accomplishment will crumble into dust.

Teiresias' parting words (447–467), announcing that the murderer is in Thebes, a non-citizen and yet a true citizen, father and brother to his children, seem to spell out what until now he has only darkly hinted at, anticipating and announcing what Oedipus will slowly discover and thereby spoiling the play's build-up of dramatic tension. If an audience's foreknowledge gives the impression that Teiresias is clearly announcing the truth, if this is allowed to usurp Oedipus' complete ignorance of any such a possibility, then it might seem that Oedipus must surely understand what is being said, thus short-circuiting the drama's inexorable movement towards a revelation of the truth. One way of dealing with what might appear to be theatrically implausible is to suppose that Oedipus does not hear these words, having turned away at 446 to enter the palace after ordering Teiresias' attendant to lead the blind man away. This seems unlikely because there is a clear sense of Teiresias directly addressing Oedipus and the dramatic force of this final encounter between the two men is heightened considerably by having them face one another: one is a fail old man, blind yet seeing the truth and alluding to it; the other is a healthy adult, capable of seeing with his eyes but blind to the truth of what is being said. Their previous conversation has been characterized by Oedipus' incomprehension and his dismissal of Teiresias as a riddling fool at best, a conspirator at worst, and the theatrical tension that arises from this fact can be seen to reach its zenith as the prophet's final words fail to register with his interlocutor. Ancient Greek and modern audiences alike cannot be surprised by what Teiresias says but the transparency of the prophet's remarks is evident only to those who already know the basic facts. For Oedipus, who knows nothing at this stage, what he hears is as riddling as the puzzle posed by the Sphinx, but this time he cannot solve it and the audience's engagement comes from the dramatic surprise at witnessing the spectacle of Oedipus hearing the truth but not registering its meaning; the truth is so close, it is spoken aloud, but rendered opaque by the enigmatic language used to express it. The frisson of such a moment would be lost if the prophet's words were addressed to the departing back of Oedipus.

The first stasimon (463–512)

The first strophe (463–473) of this choral ode speculates about the identity and circumstances of the murderer proclaimed by the oracle of Apollo in Delphi. Someone is guilty of an utterly unspeakable crime and flight now becomes his only option –

> The hour is coming when more powerfully
> Than horses moving like the stormwinds he
> Must move his feet to flight.[4]

– because the son of Zeus (Apollo) and avenging goddesses will pursue him. The word that Sophocles uses for these avenging spirits of the dead (*kēres*) may refer not so much to specific spirits, like the Erinyes that appear in Aeschylus' *Eumenides*, but to a more general sense of doomed misfortune (hence 'the Fates' that appear in a number of translations of these lines).[5]

This sense of a foretold doom is evident in the first antistrophe (474–482) with its sympathy for the situation of the fugitive. The expression of sympathy for the killer comes as a surprise given the nature of the crime but it is more understandable if read as signifying pity for the plight of the outlaw as a hunted individual, an outcast from the *polis*, wandering like an animal amidst rocks and in woods, seeking refuge in caves. This is the dread that the chorus can empathize with, the awful predicament of a man fleeing from the judgement of the oracle, yet never able to be rid of it. Such a predicament, of course, is that of Oedipus: he fled the *polis* where he had been brought up in a vain attempt to keep a safe distance between himself and the oracle that he would kill his father.

In the second strophe and antistrophe, the chorus expresses its dilemma after hearing Oedipus criticized by a seer whose prophecies would seem to have their source in some divine force. Teiresias is also a mortal and there is no sure test that could determine whether he is more knowledgeable than another man. For the time being, Oedipus has the advantage because his wisdom has been clearly seen from the encounter with the Sphinx (*phanera* in line 507 and *ōphthē* in the following line, both come from verbs of seeing) whereas the seer is making unsubstantiated 'blind' accusations. The chorus is confused, but concludes (511) by placing trust in their *phrenos*, taking Oedipus to be innocent of the accusations made against him by Teiresias. The judicious use of *phrenos*, translated by Jebb as 'heart', by Grene as 'mind' and by Lloyd-Jones as 'judgement', is interesting because of the way *phrēn* straddles the emotional and the rational. The usual Greek word for the mind's rational capacity is *noos* (from which is derived the English 'nous') and for 'spirit' or 'soul' *thumos*, while *phrēn* occupies a middle ground between the two. In the way that Greek words like these relate to parts of the physical body, *phrēn* refers to the diaphragm but signifies the heart or mind as a seat of thought and the word is used by Sophocles to refer to a faculty of reasoning. All three words relate to psychological functions although there is disagreement about how consistently or knowingly they can read as part of a theory of the mind.[6] What seems clear here, though, is that the chorus feels both intellectually and emotionally drawn to the side of Oedipus in his conflict with Teiresias even though a part of the chorus is worried by the godlike ability of the seer to prophesize.

Oedipus and Creon (513–630)

Creon, having heard that Oedipus has accused him of involvement in the murder of Laius, arrives to defend himself. He addresses Oedipus as *ton tyrannon* (514), a ruler not related through a blood line to the previous king, setting the tone for the highly political nature of this *agon*. Oedipus comes across as impatient and annoyed, but firmly in control. He readily acknowledges his suspicions: after all, it was Creon, the brother of the queen and the man most likely to rule were Oedipus removed from power, who suggested sending for Teiresias (288). He senses a conspiracy at work and behind the hariolations of the seer there is a concerted plan to oust him; he knows well that he must act swiftly in order to crush the plot:

> When he that plots against me secretly
> moves quickly, I must quickly counterplot.
>
> (618–619)

This is the language of *Realpolitik* and it demands that the threat be dealt with by putting Creon to death; the implication being that sending him into exile would not remove the possibility of further plotting.

Creon is cautious and reasons with his accuser by calmly pointing out that he is not attracted to the idea of being king; he has many of the benefits of a ruler, but without the anxiety and responsibilities that being sole ruler would entail. Oedipus is not impressed and the growing intensity of their argument is reflected in the *antilabē* (page 21) that is only brought to an end by the chorus' interruption announcing the arrival of the queen.

Up until this moment (631–633), Jocasta has not been named as the wife of Oedipus. The first reference to his marriage came when he mentioned how he had dispatched his brother-in-law to consult the oracle at Delphi (69–70), but this did not establish that he is still married to Creon's sister and it allowed for the possibility that he is referring to another sister, the one that in one version of the story he married after the death of Jocasta (page 4). There was also a possible ambiguity in the scene where Teiresias told Oedipus that he is the killer of Laius and that incest has been committed. When, now, Creon defends himself by pointing out how he and his sister, along with Oedipus himself, are more or less equal in power (so why go to the trouble of trying to usurp Oedipus?) and states that Oedipus is married to his sister (577), a similar ambiguity could surround his words because he might be referring to the other sister that Oedipus might have married after Jocasta's death. According to this reading it is only when the chorus names Jocasta as the woman coming out from the palace that the dramatic ambiguity is resolved: 'Sophocles, having toyed with us for so long, finally lays his first card on the table by making it clear to us at last who Oedipus' wife actually is'.[7]

Jocasta, Oedipus and Creon (631–678)

Jocasta and Oedipus are seen together for the first time and this is going to be a dramatic moment because of the audience's awareness of their incestuous relationship and the fact that Oedipus and Jocasta themselves are unaware of this. Her entrance is especially theatrical if the audience cannot be sure if Jocasta is still alive until the moment she appears and the chorus announces her identity (631–633). What can be said with certainty is that this is the first time in the play that all three actors are present, along with the chorus, and the interchange of song and speech gives the moment its own unique dramatic intensity.

The sense of almost naive innocence initially created by her brisk manner in breaking up the two men's row, reminding them of the larger situation and calling on them to retire inside the palace is swiftly replaced by the grim irony of her final line (*kai mē to mēden algos eis meg' oisete*), aptly translated by Grene: 'Don't magnify your nothing troubles'. What seems to Jocasta to be a 'nothing' (*to mēden*) will soon, with her help, be revealed as anything but, something that Creon unconsciously touches on by the mention of Oedipus' name in the same line (639) of his first address to his sister as 'of the same blood' (*homaime*).

Creon swears his innocence and puts himself under his own curse (644), should he be proved guilty of the charge brought against him. Both Jocasta and the chorus refer to his oath as evidence of his innocence when pleading on his behalf, leaving Oedipus to point out the terrible consequences for himself should they be mistaken. If Creon is conspiring against the king, it is Oedipus who will be banished or killed. The chorus responds with a heartfelt plea on behalf of the *polis* and Oedipus very reluctantly agrees to let Creon go. The parting words of Creon, noting his brother-in-law's gracelessness, are telling: 'natures like yours are justly heaviest for themselves to bear' (675). Oedipus is who he is, it is his nature (*phusis*), and this will prove to be his undoing as well as the source of his worth.

Jocasta and Oedipus (679–862)

In the opening exchange between Jocasta and the chorus a reluctance can be discerned on Oedipus' part to relate to his wife what has taken place with Teiresias and then Creon. Jocasta obviously wants to know what the argument has been about, but Oedipus says nothing to her until she begs him 'by the gods' (*pros thēon*). He tells her that he has been accused by her brother of killing Laius but Creon did not make this accusation. Oedipus has jumped to the conclusion that because Creon suggested bringing in Teiresias, the two of them must be conspiring against him. Thus Creon is behind the claim by the prophet Teiresias that Oedipus is the killer of Laius and, accordingly, Oedipus concludes that Creon is making this accusation. He does not explain this reasoning to his wife and her question (704) – whether Creon knows this for himself or heard it from someone else – concerns only the basis for his accusation. An uncanny irony unfolds when, hearing that the source of the accusation comes from a prophet, she tries to reassure him that there is nothing to worry about because she can demonstrate the limitations of prophets and their predictions. She tells him how a prophecy that Laius would be killed by his own child was dealt with by having their three-day-old baby abandoned in a remote location. The infant, with its ankles pinned together, could not have survived to become one of the robbers who killed Laius 'at a place where three roads meet'. For the third time in the play, first the oracle that Creon brought from Delphi, then the arrival of the seer Teiresias and now Jocasta's tale, something happens that is expected to bring relief only for the intention to reverse itself into an undesirable result. It is the mention of Laius being killed where three roads meet that causes turmoil in Oedipus' *phrenos* (mind or heart) and a deep disquiet (*psukhēs planēma*), 'a wandering of the soul' in Grene's literal translation.

From this point on, nothing is ever the same again. The mention of the three roads has triggered a memory in Oedipus and shifted irrevocably the axis of his concerns. The affliction besetting Thebes, initially channelled into the need to establish who killed Laius, recedes into the background by a process of displacement arising from the pivotal narratives delivered first by Jocasta and then Oedipus.

Jocasta is not aiming to be revelatory in her account of the past; there is a horrible contingency at work, one that goes to the heart of the drama, shown here in the way her intention to offer comfort, by examples of falsifiable oracles, becomes by accident the means of unfolding an awful horror. She attributes details of the story, where and how Laius was killed, to rumour, using a word (*phatis*) that can also mean 'a voice from heaven', 'the voice of an oracle' – the word is used in this sense earlier in the play (151 and 310). As with the effect of her intention to proffer reassurance, her use of a word with this double meaning enacts a reversal, this time one that is reflected back into language itself. She wanted to reassure Oedipus, but accidentally creates mental turmoil for him; she wanted to attribute details of Laius' death to rumour, but accidentally associates it with predestination.

Oedipus, startled by his wife's narrative, responds first (738) with a heartfelt expression of vulnerability – 'What have you designed, O Zeus, to do with me? (the only mention of Zeus other than by the chorus) – but quickly recovers his composure and, like a detective, seeks basic spatial and temporal information regarding the scene of a crime. The answers to his forensic questioning perturb him deeply and lead to another question: 'tell me of Laius – How did he look?' (740). The word he uses here for Laius' appearance, *phusis*, is the same word that Creon used when referring to Oedipus' nature (675), provoking the thought that in asking about Laius he is also asking about himself. Such a thought is contained in Jocasta's reply: Laius, she remarks, looked a little like Oedipus. At this pivotal moment, the importance of the sole witness to the killing asserts itself. First brought to attention by Creon ('. . . all were killed save one', 118), the witness now comes back into the field of evidence ('who was it told you this?', 754).

The autobiographical narrative by Oedipus begins by switching the audience's attention from Thebes to the city of Corinth where Polybus was his father and Dorian his mother. Rankled by rumours that he is not his father's son, he travelled to Delphi to consult the oracle and establish an authoritative denial of the gossip concerning his parentage. Dramatically, this third and final account of a visit to an oracle is the most explosive of all. There is no known account before Sophocles of such a visit to Delphi by Oedipus, so this moment in the drama came as a surprise to the first audience and, unlike the previous two oracles, the words of Apollo are addressed directly to the person they concern. They did not tell him what he came there to know, for his parentage was not confirmed, and instead pronounced something more terrible than he could possibly have expected: children would be born from his incest with his mother, he was told, and he would kill his own father.

Oedipus' account of what happened where the three roads meet is succinctly reported and it was seemingly an act of manslaughter. Nonetheless, it was a killing that now targets him as the likely recipient of the curse he pronounced on the killer of Laius. It is not a moral or legal issue surrounding the killing that concerns Oedipus, but the objective consequences it may entail. With the conjunction 'if', he holds out the possibility that the man he killed was not Laius –

> If it happened there was any tie
> of kinship twixt this man and Laius,
>
> (813–814)

– but the attention of the audience, knowing this is a shred of comfort that he will soon be forced to relinquish, is more likely to be aroused by the complicity of 'kinship' and 'Laius' in his words. They point to the true nature of the kinship, not the possible identity of 'this man' as Laius, but the relationship between the man killed and the man's son.

Oedipus is unaware of this relationship, he does not know what the audience knows, and his worry at this stage is limited to the possibility that he killed a stranger who was in fact the king of Thebes. He has not made a connection between the prophecy that he would kill his father, the prophecy that Laius would be killed by his son and the likelihood that he killed Laius. This is psychologically surprising, but theatrically effective; dramatic pace is maintained by slowing down the process of Oedipus' full recognition of what has taken place. The pain that will come from such a recognition is prolonged by having it slowly reveal itself, a prolongation that is enacted in the imprecision of Jocasta's reference to the binding or yoking (*enzeuxas*) of her child's feet; the inexactness allows for the failure of Oedipus to make the connection with his own lameness.

Oedipus feels aghast at the thought of having killed a man and then taken his place in the marital bed, a misery compounded by thinking that if he does have to leave Thebes, as a victim of his own curse that banished from the land whoever killed Laius, he cannot return to his family in Corinth. He feels he must avoid this at any cost in order to avoid fulfilling the prophecy he heard about himself at the oracle. The ironies increase: replacing Laius in Thebes is not what he needs to worry about, just as he need not strive to avoid returning to Corinth. In both cases, the damage has been done. The three oracles overlap in horribly ironic ways and combine to create a claustrophobic sense of imprisonment; possible escape routes are only mirages, apparently offering a means of breaking out, but only serving to tighten the net that encloses and confines him. The first oracle stated that the killing of Laius must be avenged if the city is to be saved and in order to try and fulfil this demand Oedipus laid a curse on whoever is responsible. The second oracle, as recounted by Jocasta, has led to the realization that it is he who killed Laius and so must depart from Thebes. The third oracle is one that Oedipus wants to avoid fulfilling but, like the second one, the events it foretold have already taken place.

At this stage, Oedipus' limited knowledge leads him to think he has most probably killed the former king of Thebes. Therefore, he has to be banished from the city, yet cannot return to his family in Corinth because of the risk of killing his father and marrying his mother. He rhetorically asks himself: 'Was I not born evil?' (*ar' ephun kakos*) (822) using for 'born' the aorist form of a verb meaning 'to grow, bring forth' (*phuein*). This is the verb from which *phusis* comes, the word that has been used earlier by Creon when referring to Oedipus' nature (675) and then by Oedipus when asking about Laius' physical looks (740). Now, unaware of the full weight of meaning behind the words – as if the killing of a man unrelated to him and the need to avoid returning to

Corinth were the very worst of his worries – he applies the word to himself. He goes on to ask (828) if it is not the case that some 'malignant God' (*ōmou tauta daimonos*) is victimizing him. The word translated here as God (*daimon*) can refer to an individual deity, but its more abstract sense, defined in Liddell & Scott's Greek–English dictionary as 'the power controlling the destiny of individuals': hence, one's lot or fortune', seems more appropriate and resonant here.

Oedipus, clinging to the value of rationality, has one hope. One servant witnessed and survived the killing of Laius and his men (even though Oedipus thought he had killed everyone there) and it seems he is still alive. After returning to Thebes this witness expressed a wish to leave the city and become a herdsman of sheep. If he is found and if he confirms the account Jocasta remembers him giving – that there were 'killers' of Laius (715–716) and not a single slayer – then there is a good chance that others were responsible and not Oedipus: 'One man cannot be the same as many', it is a matter of arithmetic, a precise reckoning of numbers. Already, though, when applied to the identity of the witness, such a plain arithmetic has begun to slip for at first he was a servant (*oikeus tis*, 756) in the royal household but now he is a herdsman looking after sheep (*poimniōn*, 761). The man that Creon first mentioned is the same man Jocasta now describes and, it will come to pass, he has another crucial role to play in the events of Oedipus' life.

Teiresias' parting shot to Oedipus, 'Go within, reckon that out' (460) echoes in the background. Oedipus is hanging on to a slim chance for if the witness reports there was only one killer, then without doubt 'the burden of the guilt inclines towards me' (847). The verb he uses (*rhepon*), carrying the sense of 'falls' or 'sinks', allows for the image of a weighing scale or balance that could easily sink one way or the other: 'then at once the balance tilts towards me' in one translation (Lloyd-Jones), 'the scales tilt, and this deed must be mine' in another (McAuslan). Oedipus feels that his fate is precariously balanced, but the audience, knowing his fate is sealed, may feel that the scale was never in a state of equilibrium to begin with.

This scene ends with the empirically minded Oedipus, still the detective hunting out clues and evidence, issuing orders for the witness to be brought to the palace, and Jocasta placing trust in her disavowal of the second oracle. Even if the servant were to change his story, she reasons, the prophecy that Laius would be killed by his own son cannot have come about because their son was abandoned and left to die on a mountain. She refers to her 'dead' son as *dustēnos* (855), a word that means 'unfortunate', but his poor luck is not due to his death as an infant, but to his life as an adult – and, unknowingly, he stands before her.

The second stasimon (863–910)

This is the third choral ode (the first [151–215] occurred after Creon's return from the oracle at Delphi; the second [463–512] after the scene between Oedipus and Teiresias) and in terms of a realist aesthetic one can imagine it occupying the time it takes for the all-important herdsman to arrive and, one assumes, state whether Laius was killed by one man or a group. It is also a solemn and reverent prayer calling for ethical clarity in the face of uncertainty and confusion. Oedipus is a ruler who has gained tremendous respect from the citizens of Thebes and yet oracles are coming to light that portend terrible deeds, oracles whose veracity have been questioned by Jocasta.

The first strophe calls up and promises faithful allegiance to a timeless, noumenal order of divine laws 'begotten in the clear air of heaven', laws not created by man on earth, not subject to change. The vocabulary of these lines echoes the secular concerns of the play through the mention of 'father', 'birth' and 'begotten' but the chorus uses them in reference to the sublimity of a celestial order (its loftiness evoked by the word *hupsipodes* [866], literally 'high-footed') that terrestrial mortals like themselves (with their feet, even the pierced ones of Oedipus, on the ground) strive to emulate in their earthly existence.

The antistrophe begins with a famous Sophoclean line about hubris engendering the tyrant (*hubris phuteuei turannon*): an excess of hubris leads inevitably to a downfall and 'there its feet are no service'. Are these lines referring to Oedipus as a tyrant in the throes of hubris? He is indeed a tyrant in the morally neutral sense that the Greek word *turannon* allows for and, moreover, became one by killing the former king who by contrast was never a tyrant. There is also the fact that he has been seen to behave in an aggressive and high-handed manner with Creon, to the point of threatening his life on the slenderest of circumstantial evidence. If the chorus' judicious homily is reduced to an ethical judgement on Oedipus, it would register a very abrupt change of attitude on its part. Nor would such a reading take into account the lines (879–880) in which the chorus counterbalances its moral maxim by acknowledging a positive aspect to the enterprising spirit of the hubristically inclined ('the eager ambition that profits the state'). What the chorus is expressing in this antistrophe is more an expression of confusion over the course of events than a sudden reversal of opinion towards a man who did not seize power in Thebes but was offered it as an unasked for gift (384).[8]

A sense of perplexity governs the second strophe as the members of the chorus call for divine justice in the face of wanton hubris and disrespect for the 'shrines of Gods' (886). If such impiety becomes socially acceptable, it concludes, 'why should I honour the Gods in the dance?' (896). What is arresting about this declaration is that it is spoken by members of a chorus as they themselves dance as part of an act of worship to Dionysus, the god celebrated in the very festival which the performance of dramas are a part of. If this line is intended to be as self-reflexive as it seems to be, then Sophocles, by drawing attention to the theatrical fiction being enacted may be drawing the audience's attention to a very real, non-fictional, concern about prevailing attitudes towards religion (see page 8).

The ode's second antistrophe comes across as an earnest wish for clarity. There is anxious uncertainty behind their remark about oracles concerning Laius being 'old and dim and men regard them not', presumably a reference to the one that Jocasta mentioned in order to demonstrate its lack of fulfilment. If Jocasta's scepticism is justified, then 'Apollo is nowhere clear in honour'. Confronted with the dire implications of such a possibility, the chorus looks for certitude and the authority of oracles as expressions of divine will. The chorus' last line (910) is a stark one (*errei de ta theia*): 'the power of the gods is perishing' (Lloyd-Jones). This is a dramatically and religiously powerful statement, creating tension for what might happen next.

The Messenger from Corinth
(911–1086)

The scene before the last one concluded with Oedipus issuing orders for the summoning to Thebes of the herdsman who witnessed the killing of Laius. When someone new now appears, an audience is likely to assume that this is the herdsman in question. Instead, he is a stranger looking for Oedipus and asking for directions to the palace. What follows this initial surprise, with all three actors on the stage, is a dramatically arresting *stichomythia* (line-by-line dialogue) in the form of a question-and-answer session between Oedipus and the stranger from Corinth, one that delays its poetic tautness by beginning with a disarming exchange of pleasantries and the messenger's enigmatic but politely intended announcement that he brings news that will give pleasure and perhaps a little pain as well. This becomes an insistently dour irony on Sophocles' part as the scene unfolds to reveal an unwelcome surprise lurking unknowingly within the news that the messenger so cheerfully delivers.

It could be said, speaking very strictly, that this is not a messenger scene because the traveller from Corinth is bringing news of a rumour (940) and not, as is the traditional role of the messenger, reporting on an event to which he is an eye-witness. As if to herald an ambivalence that will attach itself to the Corinthian's news, when Oedipus asks how Polybus died (960) he receives, as will be seen, a reply couched in a metaphor and Oedipus has to interpret this: 'So he died of sickness, it seems' (961). The deeper ambivalence, of course, arises from the nature of the surprise that the messenger unwittingly brings to Oedipus.[9]

Before either the messenger or Oedipus appears, Jocasta has entered carrying garlands and this could be staged to appear as a visual reminder of the play's opening scene. She comes as a suppliant to the god Apollo, gesturing presumably to the altar in the middle of the *orchestra* at line 919 ('. . . as suppliant to you, Lycaean Apollo'), but, once again, it is Oedipus who occasions the act of supplication. What has taken place in the meantime, however, renders the present moment and the state of Oedipus crucially different. It is not a gathering of citizens beseeching their king for help but the king's wife offering supplication on his behalf because, given Oedipus' state of mind, it is he who now needs help. Oedipus' normal state of mind – decisive, lucid, full of confidence – was demonstrated in the opening scene but his wife now describes someone whose mental state has reversed itself. Once calm, he now 'excites himself too much'; once rational, he is now incapable of 'conjecturing like a man of sense, what will be from what was'; and where once he was in control he is now 'always at the speaker's mercy'.

What we hear in Jocasta's words is a description of a man in the grip of fear, someone whose nous has deserted him, a person who mentally has undergone a reversal. The kernel of a proper tragedy for Aristotle is a recognition or discovery (*anagnōrisis*) and a reversal (*peripeteia*), but the kind of reversal that alarms Jocasta here is not what Aristotle has in mind, and for good reason. Oedipus has not undergone the kind of mental reversal that Jocasta's description points to and it is more her fear that is coming to the surface here. Oedipus is in a state of tremulous uncertainty and expectation and he is experiencing some fear, but he is not as much shaken as his wife. Jocasta fears that the helmsman is no longer in control of his vessel, a nautical image that harks back to earlier ones of this kind (23–24 and 694–696), but it is about to be shown that Oedipus has not lost his mental bearings and it is his wife who struggles to control the advancing storm. The reversal that is taking place, and the one that Aristotle clearly has in mind, arises from the disjunction between the good news that the messenger thinks he is bringing to Thebes – the death of Polybus and the likelihood that Oedipus will be the new king of Corinth – and the harrowing consequences that will follow in the wake of his revelations about Oedipus' origins.

Returning to the arrival of the messenger, his news brings relief and joy to Jocasta and her husband. The news could not have come at a better time, even though it does not affect the probability that it was Oedipus who killed Laius at the place where three roads meet. This, though, is not what is uppermost in their minds because what does lighten their gloom is that the death of Polybus establishes the susceptibility of oracles to error:

> As for the oracles that faced me, Polybus has gathered them up
> And lies in Hades with them – they're not worth anything.
>
> (971–972)

McAuslan's translation here captures the sense of closure that brings such relief to Oedipus. If an oracle has been proved false in one respect then, he wants to believe, the very concept of an oracle is open to doubt. What oracles say is bound to take place need not happen because everything comes down to chance and not fate. This is the comfort that Jocasta draws from the messenger's news while she waits for Oedipus to arrive: 'Now he [Polybus] is dead – and Chance, not he, is the cause' (949, McAuslan's translation). Contingency (*pros tēs tukhēs*) is the opposite of fate and even though this means that something terrible can occur just as readily as something joyful, it is the unpredictability that frees Oedipus from the burden of gloom that he has carried with him since he first heard the oracle announce he would kill his father and have sex with his mother. The messenger bears witness to the changeable nature of life when, questioned as to how Polybus died, he replies (961): 'The old are laid to rest by a small tilt of the scales' (McAuslan translation). The word here that carries the sense of a downwards inclination of a scale (*rhopē*) comes from the same verb that Oedipus used (849) to convey the critical importance of establishing whether one or more than one person killed Laius (page 68). Chance is everything and what determines an outcome may be a small but vital happenstance.

Even though the fact of Polybus' death has laid to rest one part of Oedipus' worries about the oracle he heard at Delphi, his initial euphoria is quickly followed by a gnawing uncertainty about the other part of the oracle concerning his mother. In response to the messenger's curiosity, Oedipus repeats the oracle (994–996), twice previously brought to Jocasta's attention (791–793, 825–827), making clear why he left Corinth. The messenger thinks he can reassure him with the information that Polybus was not his real father but the audience knows that this will prove the most unwelcome news when Oedipus is made aware that his parentage does not lie in Corinth. Reassurance to Oedipus can only come from knowing that his father was in Corinth and that he is now dead. The news that Polybus is dead, but that he was not his father will bring no comfort and only intensify Oedipus' need to establish the truth.

A crucial turning point in the conversation between Oedipus and the messenger becomes a supremely theatrical moment in lines 1006–1007. The enterprising messenger has not travelled to Thebes as an official representative of the Corinthian state but as a private citizen who hopes he will be rewarded for informing Oedipus that he is likely to be offered the kingship now that his father Polybus has died. At this stage, he readily admits, his news is only gossip (940), but he feels sure this is what will come to pass. In the same spirit of honesty, when Oedipus thanks him for the news, he acknowledges his motive:

> Why, it was just for this I brought the news – to earn your thanks when you had come safe home
>
> (1006–1007)

Their conversation could have stopped here or taken a different turn but, instead, the messenger's remark about returning home prompts Oedipus to state that he will never return to Corinth and it is this resolve that in turn prompts the messenger to reveal that Polybus was not his father. This leads to the revelation that Oedipus was found as an infant on the slopes of Cithaeron with his feet 'pierced and fettered'. The person most immediately affected by this information is Jocasta and her silence as the conversation between Oedipus and the messenger continues is pregnant with meaning. Although she says nothing at this stage, it is very possible that some gesture or movement on the part of the actor playing Jocasta conveys to the audience the momentous significance this moment has for her. It becomes clear from what is said when her silence is finally broken that the awful truth has dawned in her consciousness during the conversation that follows the mention of Cithaeron and pierced feet. Thus the audience watches Oedipus cross-examining the messenger, and incorrectly surmising from the answers that he may be of low birth, while Jocasta, an audience of one on the stage, watches the same scene and correctly concludes that it is her son who is standing beside her.

Oedipus himself seems unaware of his wife's presence at this stage for all his attention is focused on what the messenger can reveal about the strange events surrounding his infancy. This leads to another vital piece of new information, the fact that it was not the messenger who found the child but a shepherd working for the then king of Thebes. Oedipus the detective probes further and this leads to the chorus identifying the shepherd as the herdsman who has been summoned to give evidence about the killing of Laius that he witnessed. Only now does Oedipus turn his attention to his wife and she is desperate to head off any further inquiry into past events. The past is now looming more heavily over them than at any previous stage but while one of them is dreadfully anxious to forestall any further information coming to light the other is buoyed up by the possibility of solving what has become a mystery not only about his part in the killing of Laius but the question of his very identity. Their priorities, though sharing a common foundation, are completely at odds with one another and their exchange of words before Jocasta leaves in despair exposes the gulf between them, between ignorance and knowledge. 'With such clues I could not fail to bring my birth to light' utters an excited Oedipus but Jocasta begs him to give up the searching for clues. Oedipus mistakenly believes this is because she is upset at the thought of her husband proving to be of low birth and dismisses her concerns. The gap between Jocasta's knowledge and Oedipus' lack of it elicits profound sympathy on his wife's part and she can only hope that his misfortune (*duspotmos*) never becomes known to him: 'Ill-fated one, may you never find out who you are!' (1068).

At the start of the play Oedipus showed his concern for the worries of the suppliants who gathered outside the palace. 'I know that you are all sick' (*oid' hoti noseite pantes*), he said, and his solidarity with them arose from a sharing of their plight: 'yet there is not one of you, sick though you are, that is sick as I myself' (59–61). Now, as Jocasta pleads with him to call a halt to any further inquiry, 'sickness' is referred to once again although not all translations make this clear. McAuslan's version of her words 'Enough that I am sick' (*halis nosous' egō*) does, however, make this obvious and it serves as a reminder of what set the drama in motion in the first place. The disease afflicting Thebes has crystallized for the moment in the sickness affecting Jocasta, an illness that comes from her knowledge that the naming of Oedipus was also the key to his identity.

The first act of naming in this scene occurs early on when the chorus explains to the messenger who the woman by their side is: 'This lady is his wife and mother of his children' (928). This is the truth, though the full truth lies unspoken in their words 'his wife and mother' (*gunē de mētēr*). The messenger politely responds by referring to her as a 'complete wife' (*pantelēs dammar*). With the messenger's recall of the infant's pierced ankles and the consequent act of naming – 'So that from this you're called your present name' – Jocasta realizes Oedipus is her son. In hearing how the abandoned infant was named, Jocasta has established Oedipus' identity, but this is the one thing she will withhold from him. Her final words bestow another name on Oedipus, a name that refers to but does not specify his identity:

> O Oedipus, unhappy Oedipus!
> that is all I can call you, and the last thing
> that I shall ever call you.

> (1071–1072)

Early on in the drama, when resolving to establish the identity of the killer, Oedipus spoke of finding a clue (220–221, see page 55) and used a word, *sumbolon*, that carried the sense of a token of identity. Now, despite the disclosures of the Corinthian messenger, Oedipus' identity continues to elude him although he feels he is on the cusp of discovering who he is, given the clues that have emerged. The word he uses in this line (1059) for a clue (*sēmeia*) was employed by Jocasta (710) when she sought to disprove the veracity of oracles with the example of the one that was reported to Laius, informing him that he would die by the hand of his own son. In response to this prophecy their child was abandoned and left to die, seemingly preventing the prophecy ever being fulfilled and this, Jocasta reasoned, was a sign (*sēmeia*), a mark, by which it can be known that oracles can be invalidated. Now, having heard the messenger's account of the infant with the pierced feet, she has received an indubitable sign that her earlier reasoning was mistaken, the fulfilment of the prophecy was not prevented, and her husband is also her son.

This pivotal scene comes to an end with the chorus exclaiming surprise at the way Jocasta has fled and Oedipus defiantly asserting his resolve to establish his identity. He sees himself as 'a child of fortune' (*paida tēs Tukhēs*), using the word Jocasta uttered (*pros tēs tukhēs*, 949) to explain the unexpected good news from the Corinthian messenger. She used the word again (977) after Oedipus, having arrived and heard the news for himself, expressed relief at the apparent refutation of one half of the oracle (that he would kill his father), but admitted to still feeling concern over the second half (that he would have sexual intercourse with his mother): 'Why should man fear since chance (*tukhēs*) is all in all' she rhetorically asks, before following though the logic of this statement: if the future is a matter of pure contingency, there is no point in unduly worrying about possible outcomes. Oedipus has firmly rejected his wife's advice to cease inquiring into his origins but now just as firmly agrees with her view that everything comes down to luck. In another grimly ironic statement of the truth, he proclaims that chance is his 'mother' and nothing can diminish his determination 'to find the secret of my birth' (1085).

The third stasimon (1086–1109)

The actor playing the part of Jocasta, having left the stage in ominous silence, has to have time to change his mask and costume and prepare for a very different role: no longer a royal female, he will reappear as a mere slave, the herdsman to whom the queen gave the baby Oedipus. The third stasimon serves a practical purpose by giving sufficient time for this important change to take place.

This is the fourth choral ode and its joyful mood contrasts sharply with the solemnity of the previous one (863–910). The grave uncertainty and perplexity of the second stasimon has given way here to an elated celebration with the chorus members dedicating their dance to the mountain, Cithaeron. In the previous scene, the messenger from Corinth revealed that the infant Oedipus was found on the mountain and the chorus now addresses the mountain, personifying it 'as native to him and mother and nurse'.

The antistrophe begins with the question that has now come to dominate the drama: if Oedipus was not born to Polybus and Dorian in Corinth, who are his parents? The chorus speculates that he may well be of semi-divine origin, a love child born to a liaison between a mountain nymph and a god. Perhaps his father was the goat-god Pan, a god of shepherds and flocks and known for his lusty sportiveness. Apollo (Loxias) is mentioned as another possibility, or perhaps it was the mischievous Hermes who was born in a cave on Mount Cyllene and as a child famously stole some of Apollo's cattle. The god of boundaries, statues of Hermes (*hermai*) were set up at road junctions where boundaries needed to be marked, bringing good luck to travellers. The chorus' final suggestion for Oedipus' parentage is Dionysus, the god whose image was carried in to the theatre during the dramatic festivals of Athens so that he could watch the performances that were held in his honour.

The audience knows full well that these conjectures are all wildly off the mark and so the chorus' joyful ode becomes an ironic interlude between the revelations about Oedipus' origins coming from the Corinthian messenger and the more devastating information that is about to come to the surface.

Oedipus and the herdsman (1110–1185)

'If some one like myself who never met him may make a guess, – I think this is the herdsman' (1110). This episode begins with Oedipus seeing someone approach who he thinks may be the long-awaited witness. The word Oedipus uses here for 'guess' (*stathmasthai*) is the Greek for 'measure by rule' and it is appropriate testimony to the power of rational thought that Oedipus has all along brought to his inquiries. His rationality was mocked by Teiresias when he advised Oedipus, after prophesying to him what fate had decreed, to 'reckon that out' (460). Reckoning matters out, applying rational thought to a problem, is what Oedipus is good at and this ability is on display once again when he sees someone approaching who he thinks he has never met before.

The new arrival is identified by the chorus as the servant who worked for Laius and is recognized by the messenger from Corinth as the man from whom he received the infant Oedipus. The herdsman had been ordered to kill the infant but, instead, handed it over to the shepherd from Corinth. He was also the man who witnessed the killing of Laius and whose arrival has been awaited so as to confirm whether one person or a group was responsible for the death of the king where the three roads meet. Oedipus, then, is mistaken on two counts for thinking he has never met the man before: the two encountered one another when Oedipus was an infant and later as an adult at the crossroads.

This man who has no name, variously referred to as servant and herdsman, is asked by Oedipus to confirm his identity. Was he in the employment of Laius? 'Yes', he answers: 'no slave he bought but reared in his own house' (1123). He was a Theban bondsman, not purchased as a slave (*ē doulos ouk ōnētos*), but born in the royal household to parents who themselves were slaves. There are strange parallels between this lowly character and Teiresias: the prophet was sent for twice and is inexplicably late in arriving (289) and this slave's long-awaited arrival also seems delayed (838, 861, 1112); both are reluctant to divulge what they know; but what most oddly unites them is that they are the only two people who all along have known the truth about Oedipus. There is something uncanny about this man's involvement in Oedipus' life:

> This Theban is the man who took the infant Oedipus to 'trackless Cithaeron', who witnessed the murder in the pass, who saw Oedipus married to Jocasta. In other words, astonishingly, wildly improbably, he has been keeping company with Oedipus all of Oedipus' life.[10]

Yet this man is a mere slave and the messenger from Corinth reminds him about the time when they knew one another as shepherds on the slopes of Cithaeron. The herdsman is asked directly if he remembers their time together or not and he replies (1141): 'You speak the truth (*legeis alēthē*) although it's a long time ago (*kaiper ek makrou khronou*)'. The Grene translation leaves out 'truth' (*alēthē*), an unhelpful omission given the importance of the word to this scene and the drama as a whole. Oedipus' mission has been to establish the truth and fulfil what the oracle said needed to be done in order to remove the pollution that is wrecking Thebes. In the course of his investigation another mystery, that of his own parentage, has emerged and establishing the truth of this matter has come to dominate his concerns. The two matters, the mystery of who killed Laius and the mystery of his own identity, are not unrelated and this central fact is crystallized by a coincidence: the man who handed over a baby to the Corinthian shepherd is the man who knows Oedipus' identity and this is the same person who witnessed the killing of Laius and knows that only one individual was responsible for that deed. All this happened a long time ago and the elderly herdsman finds himself having to speak the truth about this past. The herdsman and Teiresias are the only two who know any of the important truths about Oedipus and now the herdsman, as was Teiresias earlier, is going to find himself revealing what his better judgement would keep private.

The herdsman tries his best to withhold the truth, but the messenger, in his ignorance, makes this impossible by pointing out that the infant exchanged on Cithaeron is the adult Oedipus who now stands before them:

> Look old man,
> here he is – here's the man who was that child!

> (1145)

'Death take you! (*ouk eis olethron*) Won't you hold your tongue', exclaims the herdsman, echoing the very words Oedipus used against Teiresias (430) when the blind prophet could not hold his tongue and asked Oedipus if he knew himself (415).

The truth is squeezed out of the elderly herdsman, who is forced under threat of torture and death to answer a forensic level of questioning that gradually and remorselessly exposes the deadly truth. It is worth noting that the threat of torture directed at the herdsman cannot be simply read as further evidence of Oedipus' violent temper, confirming an impression formed from his earlier conduct towards Teiresias; in ancient Athens, the evidence of a slave in a court of law was only creditable when given under torture.

The first question is whether he handed over an infant to the man who stands beside him and his affirmative response confirms the account given earlier by the Corinthian messenger. Oedipus then asks whether the infant was the herdsman's own or not and the negative response to this question produces the third question: where did the infant come from? Under duress, the herdsman admits that the child came from the house of Laius, but this still leaves open the possibility that the child's parents were not Laius and Jocasta. Oedipus therefore asks (1168), 'A slave? or born in wedlock?':

> Herdsman: O God, I am on the brink of frightful speech.
> Oedipus: And I of frightful hearing. But I must hear.

> (1169–1170)

This is the point of no return for Oedipus and the herdsman knows it. The previous question-and-answer session has been like a courtroom cross-examination or a police interrogation but the point has now been reached where the interrogator knows that the answer to his next question will most probably implicate only himself. The herdsman's reference to Jocasta (1171–1172), which may be an attempt on his part to avoid any further questions, only draws attention to the dreadful implications of what has been revealed. At this crucial moment in the episode (1173–1176) the pace of the spoken lines increases, with a change of speaker within the line leading to a rapid exchange of half-lines (*antilabē*) –

Oedipus:	She gave it to you?
Herdsman:	Yes she did, my lord.
Oedipus:	To do what with it?
Herdsman:	Make away with it.

– which continues until the doom-laden line is spoken by the herdsman: 'They [words of an oracle] said that he should kill his parent'. Jocasta, in accordance with Laius' intention to avoid the prophecy that he would be killed by his son (711ff.), gave her infant son to the herdsman so that he would not live and Oedipus replies to the confirmation of this fact with two words (*tekousa tlēmōn*): the first is an aorist feminine participle meaning 'she who gave birth' while the adjective *tlēmōn* covers 'suffering', 'patient', 'wretched', 'miserable'. This allows for some scope in translation and many versions disavow the sympathetic: 'She was so hard – its mother' (Grene), 'Her own child, the wretch?' (R. C. Jebb), 'The child's mother? How could she?' (McAuslan, virtually identical to Fagles' 'Her own child? How could she?'). What these renditions of the Greek fail to allow for is a note of pity or even compassion in Oedipus' words and the way in which he momentarily brackets off his own existence and refers to himself in the third person – after all, he himself was the child whose murder had been sanctioned by his mother – expressing feeling for the plight of a woman who found herself in an awful situation. It cannot be assumed that Sophocles intended the two words to take the form of a question rhetorically underlining Jocasta's cold-heartedness.

The oracle that Jocasta referred to when trying to reassure her husband that such prophetic utterances could be mistaken (712–714) is now mentioned by the herdsman. Oedipus, although he must by now realize that the truth of the oracle given to Laius is the same truth expressed in the oracle he heard himself at Delphi (791–794), asks one final question, dispassionately inquiring why the herdsman did not obey his orders and kill the infant. This looks as though he is tying up a loose end in the events surrounding the matter under investigation but, if so, he forgets to clear up the issue that first brought the herdsman into his enquiries, namely his evidence as the only remaining witness to what happened at the crossroads when Laius and those with him were killed. The herdsman's existence as a surviving witness was first mentioned early in the play (118–125), when Creon was being asked about the circumstances surrounding the king's death; and when Oedipus first began to suspect that he may have been the killer, he was anxious to hear what he had to say (755–766). This became imperative when the only possibility that he was not the slayer came down to the uncertainty over the number of people involved in the killing (836–850), an imperative that leads to Oedipus asking again if the herdsman has been sent for (859–861). Now, with the man finally present, the matter is not addressed, but such an omission seems understandable and explainable because the herdsman's evidence has vindicated the oracles' truth about Oedipus marrying his mother. The other part of the oracles, concerning the killing of Laius by his son, has fallen into place like the last piece of a jigsaw. He does not need empirical verification from the herdsman about what happened at the crossroads because the truth is now obvious: Oedipus killed his father and married his mother, acts of parricide and incest perpetrated in ignorance, but acts nonetheless and ones now known to he who carried them out. (As will be seen, however [see page 106], the unresolved matter of the herdsman's evidence regarding how many were involved in the altercation with Laius at the crossroads does allow for a case to be made for the possibility that it was not actually Oedipus who killed his father.)

It is left to the herdsman to state what has become obvious to everyone (1181): 'you were born ill-fated' (McAuslan). He uses the word, 'ill-fated' (*duspotmos*), that Jocasta spoke when she fled the scene before speaking for the last time to her son and husband (1068).

Oedipus realizes that all three oracles dovetail and point towards him: the oracle he heard at Delphi and the one that came to Laius were renditions of the same prophecy and the one that Creon reported, attributing the calamity affecting the city with pollution caused by the killing of Laius, points clearly to himself. Everything is now plain and distinct (*exēkoi saphē*) to Oedipus (1182); the truth is as clear as the light from the sun: 'Oh, oh! All is now clear! O light, may I look on you for the last time' (Lloyd-Jones), utters Oedipus, and the imagery of light and dark, allied to sight and blindness, reaches a tragic conclusion. At the start of the play, when Creon was seen arriving back from Delphi, Oedipus was hopeful that he brought good news 'like a bright eye' (see page 51) and towards the end of that scene he announced that 'I will bring this to light' (132). His mission has been successful and what lay buried in darkness has been brought into the light of day.

The Fourth stasimon (1186–1222)

The chorus, so ebullient in the previous ode, now reflects philosophically on the ephemeral nature of mankind in the light of what has been revealed. Can the value of life, the 'generations of men' mentioned in the first line, be ascertained or measured in some way? The chorus offers a reckoning, makes an account of it (*enarithmōu*), and the value arrived at is 'nothing' (*to mēden*). Not 'close to nothingness' (Lloyd-Jones) but, more starkly, 'how I count you ["generations of men"] as living a life that is a nothingness' (R. D. Dawe). The verb used by the chorus for its act of calculation (*enarithmōu*) is not the same as the one used by Teiresias to Oedipus, 'Go within, reckon that out' (460), and nor should it be given the difference between empirical accounting and metaphysically assessing life's value. Oedipus found confidence in the rigour of his intellect; it underpinned his ability to defeat the Sphinx, but it cannot deal with what he presently has to face and come to terms with. A very different kind of reckoning is now called for, a need posed by the chorus' question:

> Where, where is the mortal who wins more of happiness than just the seeming, and, after the semblance, a falling away?
>
> (1189–1192)

R. C. Jebb's translation expresses the poignancy captured in the fleeting transition from 'seeming' to 'after the semblance'(from the same verb *dokeō*). Happiness is only the appearance of well-being and the outward show is followed by a 'falling away', a fading of what was never substantial in the first place. The strophe comes to its own sad end with the realization that Oedipus' fate is an emblem of the human condition, the calculus yields a zero: 'I say that nothing (*ouden*) pertaining to mankind is enviable' (1194–1195, Lloyd-Jones).

As if to punish itself for its illusionary belief in happiness, the chorus reminds itself of who Oedipus was and what he represented, his achievements that had appeared so solid and permanent. The chorus notes his victory over the Sphinx, the 'taloned maid of the riddling speech', and the way he came to embody the security and protection of the *polis*: 'a tower against death for my land'. He was its true king (*basileus*, not *turannos*), but now there is no one more wretched, no one who has undergone such a change to their life (*allaga biou*). He is referred to (1207) as the 'famous Oedipus' (Lloyd-Jones), employing the same adjective (*kleinos*) that Oedipus used to describe himself at the start of the play (8), the reversal of his position registered at a grammatical level in the switch from the nominative to the accusative (*kleinon*); Oedipus is no longer the subject performing an action, but the object affected by the action. The sexual relationship with his mother is the action in the mind of the chorus, not the killing of his father, and it is referred to (1208–1211) using imagery from sea-faring (the harbour or haven) and farming (the ploughed furrow). An earlier nautical image placed Oedipus at the helm –

> When my dear land was in trouble before and adrift,
> You bought a fair wind and set her on a straight course:
> Be as good a pilot to us again now.
>
> (694–696)

– but the emphasis now is on the disastrous course that his own life took, the apparently safe harbour being the place of taboo. The awful reversal that has taken place becomes a personal source of grief for the chorus, recorded in the final lines of its ode:

> I drew my breath
> from you at the first and so now I lull
> my mouth to sleep with your name
>
> (1220–1222)

The Greek does allow for alternative translations of the last part, along the lines of R. C. Jebb's 'and through thee darkness hath fallen upon my eyes', but the intensity of the chorus' anguish remains the same.

The second messenger (1223–1296)

The expectations of an ancient Greek audience regarding a messenger's speech would seem about to be amply fulfilled when, coming out from the palace, the *exangelos* describes what he has seen and heard within. He addresses the chorus as 'ever held in greatest honour in this land' (1223, Lloyd Jones), a greeting that once might more properly have been reserved for the king and queen, but which in the circumstances is more appropriate for the Theban elders making up the chorus. The family that ruled the city belonged to the 'house of Labdacus' (the father of Laius), but this house has been ruined almost beyond redemption. The water of two great rivers, Ister (the Danube) and Phasis (the Rioni) that flow into the Black Sea, could not provide the cleansing power that would be needed by way of purification (*katharmō*) for what lies hidden in the house. The religious implications of purification work alongside the messenger's role in addressing the theatre's audience and preparing them for the spectacular nature of what is about to be revealed.

When Jocasta fled from Oedipus, after uttering her last words to him (1071–1072), she returns to the place where her tragedy began. Inside the bedroom, she slams shut the doors not to close herself off from the appalling reality of what has become clear but more as an act of withdrawal into herself and away from the knowledge that now torments her. She inflicts mental pain on herself by fixating on the bed where Oedipus was conceived and where later she lay incestuously with him, calling upon Laius to remember the time 'that night long past which bred a child for us'. The messenger can only report what he hears though the locked door of the palace bedroom and, in what has been taken as a further indication of an inadequacy in his role as knowledgeable messenger, he confesses to not knowing how she died ('How after she died I do not know', 1251).[11] At this stage, Oedipus becomes the attention of the messenger's report (1252–1254) until we return to the dead Jocasta as seen and reported by the *exangelos* (1263–1265).

Oedipus' behaviour is described by the messenger in very violent language. He bursts into (*eisepaisen*, 1252) the palace, wanting a sword and seeking his wife although it is not clear whether he intends to kill Jocasta or himself or both of them. Finding the doors of their bedroom closed, he hurls himself (*enēlat'*) against them, forcing them inwards 'wrenching the hollow bolts out of their sockets'. The brutal nature of what he sees and then what he does to himself is all the more shocking because of the vivid details in the messenger's account: Jocasta 'hanging, her neck tied in a twisted noose' (Lloyd-Jones), the 'chased brooches fastening her robe', blood from his eyes staining his beard. The verb used at 1253 to convey his violent entry into the palace is used again for the manner in which he pierces his eyes (1270). Imagery from the world of agriculture, used earlier by the chorus (1210) to describe the act of incest, also comes to the mind of Oedipus with his talk of 'this field of double sowing whence I sprang and where I sowed my children'. The natural processes of agriculture become metaphors for a violation of the natural order so transgressive that the messenger cannot bring himself to put it into words:

> He shouts
> for some one to unbar the doors and show him
> to all the men of Thebes, his father's killer,
> his mother's – no I cannot say the word.
>
> (1286–1288)

Alongside this reluctance to say a certain word is the fact that the messenger does not use direct speech in his account of what happens inside the palace. This is unusual to the point of uniqueness – no other messenger speech in Greek tragedy chooses to avoid direct speech – and underlines the inability of the messenger to enter into the narrative by taking on the part of Oedipus or Jocasta: 'The events pass in a kind of appalled silence. He holds them at a distance from himself and from us.'[12]

The messenger's long speech draws to an end, as it began, by preparing the audience for what is to follow. Oedipus wants to show himself to his city, the *polis* from which he banished himself in his proclamation, and needs assistance to make his way out from the palace. The visual attention of the audience is directed towards the palace door through which earlier Jocasta and Oedipus fled in panic; Oedipus now appears with his mask modified or with a new one, perhaps one with gaping holes where his eyes should be or one with red colouring or ribbons.

Blinded Oedipus and the chorus (1296–1422)

The chorus reacts to the sight of blinded Oedipus with a song (1296–1306) expressing shock that verges on repulsion, attributing at first his blinded state to some act of madness (*mania*, 1300) or the result of some spirit (*daimon*) having 'leaped' or sprung (*pēdēsas*) on him. Earlier in the drama, at a time when Oedipus thought his worst fate was the killing of his father, he had wondered if some *daimon* was victimizing him (828) and now such a possibility occurs to the chorus as an explanation for his ill-fated life (*dusdaiamoni moira*). Though horrified, the chorus is drawn into what has happened and wants to know more.

Up until now Oedipus has spoken in iambic trimeters, but here the dialogue is characterized by 'marching' anaepests on the part of the chorus and 'melic' anaepests by Oedipus (see page 22). The change in metre registers an alteration in Oedipus' sense of himself and the world. Angst-ridden and confused, separated from the substance of his being he has become something lightweight and flimsy, his physical loss of sight actualizing his subtraction from his known universe and the metaphysical blindness he finds himself experiencing: 'Where am I being carried in my sorrow? Where is my voice borne on the wings of the air?' (Lloyd-Jones). In the next line (1311), a *daimon* is again mentioned when conveying his sense of being catapulted out of his known world (*iō daimon, hin exēllou*). In empathy, the chorus answers his question while at the same time giving expression to the negation that has enveloped him:

> To a terrible place whereof men's ears
> may not hear, nor their eyes behold it.

Lacan's notion of 'subjective destitution', a culminating stage in the psychoanalytic process between an analyst and the analysand, is one way of approaching the point Oedipus has reached here. Without the aid of an analyst except his own traumatic experiences and the ability to dwell on what has taken place, Oedipus is able to confront the vertiginous abyss that is now his life – 'madness and stabbing pain and memory' (1316) – and avoid transferring it onto the Other (the gods, fate, Apollo). He acknowledges the big Other as the symbolic background to what has occurred, possibly gesturing towards the altar of the god Apollo as he speaks, but resists the temptation to simply shift responsibility to a divine order:

> It was Apollo, friends, Apollo,
> that brought this bitter bitterness, my sorrows to completion.
> But the hand that struck me
> was none but my own.

What happened is the result of action by his own hand (*autokheiru*), applying the same word that he used earlier for the murder of Laius (266). No one was pulling the strings when he killed his father and married his mother, or when he blinded himself. In an important sense, despite the oracles, he was foresightless. He regrets being saved from death as an infant, but now has to deal with the consequences of being alive and having brought terrible distress to those dear to him (1355, *philoisin*), hence his wish to be taken away. He is overwhelmed by a sense of his isolation, abandoned by the gods (1360, *atheos*), and concludes:

> If there is any ill worse than ill,
> that is the lot of Oedipus

> (1365–1366)

The chorus replies by saying he would better be dead than blind and its first words (*ouk oid'hopōs*) uncannily echo his name. The lot of Oedipus was a 'not knowing', his ignorance the fatal flaw in his self-lauded power of rational thinking.

Beginning at line 1369, the metre returns to iambic trimester for Oedipus' statement of intent and his anguished awareness that he is no longer *at home*.

Provoked into justifying his action, by the chorus remarking that he would be better off dead than living in his self-blinded state, Oedipus feels that he has done what was necessary. The decree he issued for the banishment from Thebes of Laius' killer (228–229, 236) will be duly implemented and, although he does not put this into words, it is the unconditional nature of this decree (and the prophecy of Teiresias (454–456) regarding Oedipus' departure from Thebes) that partly inhibits the possibility of following Jocasta in an act of suicide. What he does say that helps explain why he does not kill himself is that he cannot face having to look at his father and mother in Hades: 'those two to whom I have done things deserving worse punishment than hanging'. His blinding is a self-inflicted act of punishment for what he has done to his parents, his children, the city of Thebes and its citizens. If he could make himself deaf as well as blind he would do so, 'locking up my miserable carcase'.

In lines 1391–1408 he apostrophizes the three places that sutured his identity – Cithaeron, Corinth and the crossroads – and gave what amounted to the meaning of his existence. Shattered by the truth, he turns away from what he would like to do to himself and addresses instead these three places (apostrophe, a figure of speech in which the subject of the enunciation turns to explicitly address some person or thing, comes from the Greek for a 'turning away'), confronting the true nature of their roles in his life. Cithaeron proved deceptive and should not have allowed him to live; Corinth, similarly, provided only the semblance of a home. The city where he thought he belonged had the outward show of a healthy domicile, but beneath the appearance a wound was festering (1396, *kallos kakōn hupoulon*); the alliterative effect of *kallos* (beauty) and *kakōn* (evil) creating an oxymoronic effect which captures the contradictory, self-negating nature of his time in Corinth. The truth of his birth came into play at the crossroads, actualizing itself in the spilling of blood, but the fact was not available to him at the time and remained hidden after he arrived in Thebes and compounded his misery by an incestuous marriage. The apostrophe continues when he personifies marriage and, by doing so, is able to create a minimum distance between what the institution of marriage allowed for – 'children who were full of incest, brides who were both wives and mothers to their spouses' (Lloyd-Jones) – and his own subjective plight as the chief subject of this marriage. Ultimately, though, Oedipus accepts the fact that he is the doer of dreadful deeds and that he stands alone:

> Approach and deign to touch me
> for all my wretchedness, and do not fear.
> No man but I can bear my evil doom.

(1413–1415)

Oedipus and Creon (1423–1530)

It is not Creon's arrival that seems so surprising, although he has been absent for so long that his appearance is hardly expected, but the abrupt way in which power has passed into his hands and his unexpected silence on the tumultuous events that have so recently taken place. Instead, he instructs Oedipus to return inside the palace and avoid defiling the light of 'our Lord the Sun'. Oedipus begs for immediate banishment and, when Creon insists that they must wait to hear what the gods think should be done, points out that this was what Apollo decreed (1441). He is referring to the words of the oracle (96–98) calling for the expulsion of those responsible for the death of Laius, but Creon demurs.

Oedipus, who at the start of the drama was an object of supplication has now become a suppliant himself when he asks that Jocasta be given a proper funeral and repeats his request for exile, explaining how he wants to return to Cithaeron and die in the place where his parents had intended his death to take place as an infant. It is as if by dying in the place where his parents wanted him to perish, he can somehow play back time and begin again, ensuring this time there is no interruption to what should have been the proper sequence of events. Perhaps some such thought was in his mind because he now qualifies the idea of death:

> Yet I know this much:
> no sickness and no other thing will kill me.
> I would not have been saved from death if not
> for some strange evil fate. Well, let my fate
> go where it will.

> (1455–1458)

Oedipus has reached a philosophical level than can be compared with the thought of Hamlet towards the end of his life's drama: matters have reached some kind of resolution and there is an acknowledgement that

> if it be now, 'tis not to come; if it be not to come, it will be now;
> if it be not now, yet it will come. The readiness is all. Since no
> man, of aught he leaves, knows aught, what is't to leave betimes?
> Let be.[13]

Oedipus' 'readiness' – 'let my fate (*moira*) go where it will' – is one of patient endurance in the face of suffering and the sense that the future cannot be controlled. He has travelled a long way from the start of the play and the confident expectation that puzzles could be solved and there is something heroic about his fortitude in accepting failure. Jocasta's suicide can be seen as just as much a response to Oedipus' refusal to accept contingency (977–979) as to her shock at discovering the truth, but now, when the malign results of a particular contingency are confirmed, Oedipus chooses not to follow her in an act of suicide.

It has been established earlier in the play (implied at 261, referred to by Teiresias at 425, by Jocasta at 1247–1251 and by Oedipus at 1375–1376) that children were born to Oedipus and Jocasta, but they have remained shadowy figures up until this moment. Now he briefly mentions his sons (1459–1461) but reserves his concern for his two daughters, Antigone and Ismene, who have entered (perhaps with Creon, but only now is their presence registered by

Oedipus). He attests to the close bond he has with his daughters by stressing how he never ate separately from them (1463–1464) and acknowledges that they will never marry because of what he has done (1497–1502). He begs Creon to have some regard for their plight, but the new ruler of Thebes is very reticent. His remark that he does not speak about what he is unsure of (1520) is remarkably similar to what he said to Oedipus early on in the play (569) when defending himself against the charge of conspiring with Teiresias. Oedipus is to be separated from his daughters and let back inside his palace. Creon makes a moralistic comment about Oedipus' lack of authority and it is left to the chorus to reinforce this tone with some further moralizing judgements. As with Fortinbras at the end of *Hamlet*, this Athenian drama concludes with a compact tidying up that disconnects with the trauma and turmoil witnessed by the audience.

Although there is no consensus, some scholars have doubts about the authenticity of the play's ending. The chorus' final words (1524–1530) are the most suspect, but the scope for discussion goes back a hundred lines to the entry of Creon. R. D. Dawe argues on literary and linguistic grounds for interpolations beginning at 1424, with the entry of Creon, to 1458 where 'everything on to the end of the play is spurious, and the voice of Sophocles is heard no more'.[14] There are good grounds for thinking the chorus' final lines are textually corrupt or so inept as to be unattributable to Sophocles – Dawe overconfidently labels them 'demented balbutience' – but a choral speech is a regular ending in Sophoclean drama and the fact that the sentiment is a familiar one in ancient Greek thought is not in itself a reason for attributing it here to an interpolator.

What is true is Dawe's assertion that everything in the play leads the audience to expect the exile of Oedipus and the ambiguity in the ending that we do have leads to the unlikely possibility of the prophet Teiresias being proved wrong in his prediction (454–456). But this is only a possibility because Teiresias does not say *when* Oedipus will leave 'tapping his way before him with a stick'. As it is, the play ends with a call to prophecy, with Creon waiting to hear from Delphi before deciding what is to be done; just as the play began, with Oedipus waiting to hear what Delphi had to say about the plague engulfing his city. The ending is certainly unexpected, but it is also dramatically surprising for an audience that may be expecting Oedipus' exile. In the course of the play, characters have made their entries down the eisodos, bringing messages from and concerning the places that have shaped Oedipus' life: Delphi, Corinth and the mountain Cithaeron that lay between them. There are good reasons for thinking that the drama will end with the blind ex-king being led down one of those aisles towards Cithaeron, away from the *skene* that represents the Theban palace. Instead, in a theatrical reversal of the opening scene when Oedipus stepped out from his palace, he is led back to the palace. He ends by going home to the place where, involving the same woman, he was conceived and conceived others. The significance of different interpretations of the ending of *Oedipus* will be returned to in Chapter Six.

Notes

1 Hölderlin (2001), p. 17.

2 'The grammatical categories of language itself, the ease of shifting from masculine ["some one man", *heis tis*, in line 118] to neuter ["one thing", *hen*, in line 119) in the inflection of the pronominal adjective "one", seem to lead the investigators astray from what will finally solve the mystery. Language itself encourages their deception in pursuing what will prove, in one sense, misinformation.' Segal (1998), p. 151.

3 There is an editorial issue about some of these lines and in the McAuslan and Affleck translation, unlike the Jebb, Watling, Grene and Berg and Clay versions, they appear in brackets. See also the comments by R. D. Dawe (2006) in the Greek edition, p. 95.

4 Hölderlin (2001), p. 30.

5 'The Μοῖρα decree, the Κῆρες execute.' Jebb (2004), p. 72.

6 Williams (1994), p. 27.

7 Sommerstein (2010), p. 219.

8 The Grene translation passes over this point but in 384 Oedipus states that he was offered the rule of Thebes as an unasked for gift (*dōrēton ouk aitēton*).

9 '... tension between the messenger's ostensible news and the significant facts which this news is capable of producing, marks the exchange of

language as a contestation of the possibility of the simple, transparent transmission and reception of signals'. Goldhill (1984), p. 193.

10   Cameron (1968), p. 22.

11   Barrett (2002), pp. 197–198.

12   Gould (2001), p. 259.

13   *Hamlet*, V.ii.215–220.

14   R. D. Dawe (2006), p. 196.

CHAPTER FIVE

Critical reception and publishing history

Virtually nothing is recorded about *Oedipus'* reception when it was first performed in Athens other than that it received only the second prize, losing out to a dramatist, Philocles, of whom very little is known and none of whose work has survived.[1] No satisfactory explanation has been offered for the award of only the second prize but, while it seems surprising, there could well have been circumstances or aspects of that year's performances that affected the judges' decision.

There is also space for speculating how Sophocles' play might have been received by an audience not only acquainted with the prevailing myths about Oedipus but also with some knowledge, if only by hearsay, about other dramas involving Oedipus and Thebes. Of the six other plays entitled *Oedipus* that have been dated to the fifth century at least one of these was produced long before Sophocles' play. This was Aeschylus' *Oedipus*, produced as the second play in his trilogy of 467 (and which a young Sophocles may have watched) and what very little is known about this play from a few surviving fragments suggests that it may have been very different from Sophocles'. One fragment refers to Oedipus cursing his sons and being angry over their lack of care for him, suggesting that the play is dealing with events long after his blinding and the discovery of his parricide and incest, and there is also a

Byzantine tradition that the play involved the tale of Pelops' son, Chrysippus, being raped by Laius who consequently incurs a curse on his family.[2] The first audience that came to watch Sophocles' *Oedipus* in the theatre brought with them their acquaintance with the myth and, presumably, a degree of speculation as to how this new drama would handle the story of Oedipus. What moments in the performance occasioned surprise in an audience remains conjecture and it is equally uncertain, especially when the date of the first production remains unknown, how the play's reception might have been affected by the course of the Peloponnesian War.

What can be said with some confidence is that by the fourth century *Oedipus* was on its way to attaining the canonical status it has never relinquished, though it cannot be assumed that Aristotle's high praise, singling it out as the paradigm of all that is best about fifth-century tragedy, was universally shared by his age. What is certain is that Aristotle's eulogy played a decisive part in establishing the play's reputation during the Renaissance.

Tragic heroism

While some approaches to *Oedipus* have, for the time being at least, passed out of fashion, their influence is still sometimes felt and this is especially the case when an interpretation achieves a currency that goes beyond the confines of ancient Greek drama. Such a case is the idea that Aristotle's *harmatia* refers to a moral flaw in an individual and that the downfall of the tragic hero is inextricably linked to this. Oedipus, by this account, must possess a flaw in his nature and it must be seen to play a part in the unfortunate events of his life. A wilful temper has been identified as his moral defect and his behaviour at the crossroads with Laius seen to bear this out. According to Oedipus, the strangers he encountered arrogantly assumed he should stand aside and let them pass and he was only defending his dignity when he struck one of those who would presume the right to push him aside. This led to Oedipus being hit on the head and his just retaliation resulted in a fight and the death of the bullying strangers. From another point of view, Oedipus' behaviour suggests a headstrong man prone to bouts of ill-temper, unable to control a tendency to resort to violence. Such a trait can also be identified in the way he loses his temper not only with Teiresias but with Creon and the herdsman as well, making threats and in the case of the herdsman being on the verge of having the unfortunate slave tortured. Along similar lines, an intellectual arrogance can be spotted in his conviction that rational means will deal with all the difficulties of finding Laius' killer ('I will bring this to light again', 132) and the taunting reminder to Teiresias that it was he and not a blind prophet who solved the riddle of the Sphinx. In this vein, his words (380ff.) accusing Teiresias of conspiring with Creon to dethrone him smack of paranoia. At the very least, it might be thought, after leaving the oracle at Delphi Oedipus should have been extremely cautious about any potentially violent encounter with an older man.

An impediment facing this interpretation is that the idea of a tragic flaw is not a term common to Greek thought and, far from finding its source in *harmatia*, Aristotle does not mention the term. From this, Charles Segal feels able to assert: 'Oedipus does not have a tragic flaw. This view rests on a misreading of Aristotle and is a moralizing way out of the disturbing questions that the play means to ask. Sophocles refuses to give an easy answer to the problem of suffering.'[3] Segal can feel adamant because as John Jones makes clear in *On Aristotle and Greek Tragedy*, *harmatia* has been imported into the *Poetics* and given an interpretative force in Greek tragedy it does not possess: 'there is no evidence – not a shred – that Aristotle entertained the concept of the tragic hero'.[4] *Peripeteia* is not a personal reversal and *anagnōrisis* is not a psychological act of recognizing one's identity; both terms relate to a situation, a state of affairs that undergo change and it is the universality of mutability that matters. As seen, Aristotle defines tragedy as 'the imitation [*mimēsis*] of an action [*praxis*]' not the imitation of people; it is through the plot that *praxis* is articulated and given form so that 'the plot is the source and (as it were) the soul [*psuchē*] of tragedy'.[5] For Aristotle, *psuchē* has a dynamic vitality that informs substance and the link between plot and tragedy is seen as analogous to the relationship between the soul and substance. Aristotle regards *Oedipus* as the paragon of tragedy, displaying the close proximity between action and the human personality as a human condition rather than a state of mind, far removed from the notion of grandeur and passionate intensity defining the romantic tragic hero.

A parallax effect makes itself apparent when aspects of Oedipus' behaviour can be attributed to character traits that in themselves are polar opposites. From one point of view his stubbornness and wilfulness is dangerously edged with a violent temper;[6] from another perspective he possesses an indomitable spirit that drives him to establish the truth and this determination to know can be admired, especially when he is prepared to pay a terrible price for it. Teiresias was the first to try and restrain his curiosity but Oedipus would not oblige (320ff., 332ff., 343); Jocasta tries her best to halt his inquiries (1056ff.) but is rebuffed; the herdsman fares no better (1114ff.) and is forced to reveal what is demanded of him. When the truth is made clear Oedipus confronts it boldly and punishes himself in an act of self-blinding, unnerving the chorus which cannot understand why he did not simply kill himself. Unlike the cautious Creon, Oedipus' personality has a majesty that continues to assert itself in the face of personal ruin, evidenced by his insistence on making public his utter wretchedness (1287–1291). If Oedipus has a flaw, it can be argued, it is not emotional impulsiveness or arrogance but something noble that emerges from his strength of character and cannot be dissociated from what makes him great. In this way, Oedipus is the quintessential tragic hero: the source of the downfall of the classic tragic hero is inseparable from the quality that constitutes his heroicness and there is something tragic as well as marvellous about such a person's endeavour, an existential fidelity that will risk everything for the sake of what is ultimately regarded as the core of their being. This idea of Oedipus as an existentialist hero was argued for in an influential study by Bernard Knox, first published in 1964, *The Heroic Temper: Studies in Sophoclean Temper*. Although this book paid more attention to *Oedipus at Colonus* than *Oedipus*, it is clear that his description of the Sophoclean hero applies to the character from both plays:

> The Sophoclean hero acts in a terrifying vacuum, a present which has no future to comfort and no past to guide, an isolation in time and space which imposes on the hero the full responsibility for his own action and its consequences . . . makes a decision that springs from the deepest layer of his individual nature, his *physis*, and then blindly, ferociously, heroically maintains that decision even to the point of self-destruction.[7]

Long after existentialism had passed out of fashion and with the growing influence of structuralist anthropology and poststructuralist theories of language, a new inflection was given to the nature of Oedipus' tragic struggle with existence. In Charles Segal's *Tragedy and Civilization: An Interpretation of Sophocles*, first published in 1981, the Greek playwright is seen to be exploring the human condition and its conflicted struggle between the civilized need for order and the ever-present undercurrent of chaos and savage meaninglessness: 'the ambiguity of man's power to control his world and manage his life by intelligence'.[8] At a general level of Greek thought, this ambiguity is present in the interplay between nature (*phusis*) and law (*nomos*), savagery and civilization, while in the Greek theatre this antinomy is acted out in the role of the tragic hero struggling to position himself on a perilous axis that separates man from beast. The polarities are inherent to the nature of life, therefore irreconcilable, and in *Oedipus* this opposition is reflected in a concern with language, a system of meaning defined in poststructuralist terms:

> [language strives] to create and maintain difference in the face of chaotic sameness, and to assert warm familiarity in the face of coldly alien otherness . . . Oedipus, solver of riddles, is led to defeat by the multiple riddles of his own being until he can find with his own life a deeper answer to the Sphinx's riddle, and that not with words alone.[9]

Oedipus becomes a tragic hero for Segal because, watched by an audience seeking catharsis from the pity and fear stirred into being by his lonely suffering, there is something ultimately noble about his pursuit of self-knowledge and in this nobility Oedipus triumphs over the chaos that threatens to undermine everything that is civilized about home (*oikos*) and community (*polis*).[10]

Ritual and myth

There is an interpretation of *Oedipus*, no longer as well known as it once was, that avoids psychologizing the individual protagonist by adopting an approach to ancient drama which locates its origins in ritual and myth. This approach found expression in relation to *Oedipus* in a 1912 translation of the play by Gilbert Murray (1866–1957). Murray's verse translations of Athenian tragedies were very popular and his general understanding of the culture that produced them was influenced by the work of another classicist, Jane Harrison (1850–1928), whom he first met in 1900. Murray and Harrison and some like-minded colleagues became known as Cambridge Ritualists and their use of anthropology and ethnography informed their reading of Greek drama. In his preface to his translation of *Oedipus*, Murray construes a background to the play that has little to do with notions of fifth-century Athenian enlightenment but which point instead to a pre-classical, primitive age and its investments of meaning in practices like curses and the exposure of new-born children – practices that are associated with ideas of pollution and malignant divinities.

Murray saw drama as evolving from a ritual celebration of a seasonal god or 'yearly spirit' (*eniautos daimon*); thus the changing of autumn into winter could call forth mourning following the death of a god, while the coming of spring could be celebrated as a happy time of fertility resulting from a marriage of the gods.[11] A ritual associated with the 'yearly spirit' that has been seen as particularly relevant to interpretations of *Oedipus* is one involving the expulsion of scapegoats (*pharmakoi*). In Athens there was a festival known as the Thargelia which apparently started with the expulsion of two men, representing male and female, arrayed with garlands of figs and paraded through the city before being ceremoniously expelled. An account of this rite dating from the sixth century describes the scapegoats as being symbolically beaten on their genitals with wild plants. Scapegoats took with them from the city any threat of pollution that might injure the well-being of the community.

This is the background for a book by Francis Fergusson, *The Idea of a Theater*, and an article by Jean-Pierre Vernant, 'Ambiguity and reversal: on the enigmatic structure of *Oedipus Rex*', both of which were influential in promoting what could loosely be called an anthropological or sociological interpretation of *Oedipus*.[12] The state of plague-ridden, infertile Thebes is like the barrenness of winter and any renewal of spring is dependent on there being a scapegoat, a surrogate victim whose punishment will purge the community by perishing for the good of the social collective. Oedipus as king carries the burden of ensuring the land's return to fertility, but spring has arrived and the expected regeneration has failed to appear. Oedipus the protagonist seeks answers to the question of his personal identity but on a grander, more ritual scale he is seeking the welfare of his community. The chorus orchestrates his progress towards the point of sacrifice, marking critical stages and asking the questions that need to be asked. The chorus is the faithful conscience of the community: 'Their errand before Oedipus' palace is like that of Sophocles' audience in the theatre: they are watching a sacred combat, in the issue of which they have an all-important and official stake'.[13] For Fergusson, *Oedipus* says something important about the culture of ancient Greece in the sort of way that *Hamlet* speaks for the modern world but the myths and rituals, taken for granted by Sophocles as part of his cultural consciousness, have to be restated for the modern mind.

Vernant's article traces the ambiguities and reversals that weave their way through the drama as emblematic of a duality that attaches itself to the figure of Oedipus. He is his own riddle, the enigma that lays hidden behind the inversions of the play, but it is not Freudian psychology that can unlock the puzzle. Oedipus was defending himself when he committed parricide and his marriage to the Theban widow that led to incest was a way of consecrating the victory over the Sphinx but, regardless, and like the accused in a Stalinist show trial, he bears 'objective guilt'. His position moves between two symbolic poles of meaning:

> It is in fact by means of the axis occupied at the summit by the divine king, at its base by the *pharmakos*, that the series of reversals takes place which affects the character of Oedipus and makes of the hero the 'paradigm' of ambiguous man, of tragic man.[14]

Far from reducing Oedipus to a symbolic cipher, however, Vernant's account concludes on a humanist note by reading Sophocles' play as a questioning of a rigidly defined *polis* by having the protagonist struggle against an imposed hierarchy that would confine man within prescribed social roles. By moving from a divine-like king to the *pharmakos*, Oedipus traverses the space that would keep them apart and 'discovers himself enigmatic, without stability or a domain proper to him, without fixed connection, without defined essence'.[15]

Interpreting the ending

The difficulty with an interpretation which sees Oedipus as a scapegoat who carries the pollution out of the city is that at the end of the play he is placed under house arrest and not allowed to leave the city. Teiresias has predicted that he will be driven out of the city (417–418) and that 'he will be a beggar, poking his way with a stick, feeling his way to a strange country' (Berg and Clay, 454–456), but he did not say when this would occur. Indeed, the drama's conclusion causes a number of problems for commentators whose general interpretation of the play leads them to want, or at least expect, a different ending to the one that seems to be given. Oedipus wants to leave Thebes but Creon does not immediately grant him this wish:

> Creon: The God, not I, must grant you this.
> Oedipus: The gods hate no man more than me!
> Creon: Then what you ask they soon will give.
>
> (1518–1519)

This translation by H. D. F. Kitto continues with Oedipus seeking an affirmative commitment 'You promise this?' (*phēs tad' oun*) and Creon replying, 'Ah no! When I am ignorant, I do not speak' (1520). Grene's translation credits Creon with an even more evasive response: 'What I do not mean, I do not use to say'; a translation by Fainlight and Littman – 'I don't equivocate, I only say what I mean' – would indicate a positive response by Creon to the request, as does Fagles' 'I try to say what I mean; it's my habit', while Don Taylor renders an emphatically negative answer: 'No. I shall do what I say I will do'. The problem is that all five of these translations, which are not identical, are possible versions of the ambiguous Greek (*ha mē phronō gar ou philō legein matēn*, 1520).

What is not ambiguous is that *Oedipus* comes to an end by not ending, leaving open the question of what will now happen to Oedipus, circling back to the play's opening where people await news from the god at Delphi. Nothing in the play has prepared an audience for this indecision because the expectation has clearly been that Oedipus will now leave Thebes. In the prologue, Creon reported the oracle's announcement that the killing of Laius must be avenged by blood or exile (100–101); Oedipus' curse called for banishment (236–245) and with the realization that he may be the killer comes the knowledge that this entails his own banishment (816–820). This is why he is asking Creon to expel him. As Peter Burian deftly puts it in an article about the play's ending: 'Exile becomes Oedipus as much as mourning becomes Electra.'[16] In this article, Burian shows how critics have found in the ending a conclusion that accords with their broader understanding of what the play is about. Thus it becomes possible to find something heroic and positive in the way Oedipus does not stumble off the stage, broken and dispirited, but reconstitutes some of the forcefulness that characterized his former self by making demands on Creon. Bernard Knox puts the case for this interpretation of the play's ending in chapter five, 'Hero', of his *Oedipus at Thebes*.[17]

For Burian, however, there is no closure, no final judgement, and the uncertainty that prevails *is* the play's resolution,

> And this inconclusive conclusion sends mixed signals about what the future will hold: Oedipus' failure (so far) to achieve the desired banishment further manifests his inability to control his destiny, but at the same time his renewed self-assertion suggests that his fate cannot be encompassed even in the tremendous arc of his peripety, nor will its meaning be contained in his self-recognition and self-punishment. More than that, the play refuses to say.[18]

This liberal way of interpreting *Oedipus* provides its own kind of comfort zone for spectators/readers who are left to make their own meanings and the unresolved question of what will happen to Oedipus can also be safely parked with an observation along the lines of 'how very, very appropriate that is for a drama that is all about a man who thought he knew everything and who has proved to know nothing'.[19] This is all well and good but the ending of *Oedipus* raises hermeneutical questions that cannot so easily be accommodated. The vexed nature of interpretation that is stirred into being by the uncertain nature of Oedipus' position at the play's 'conclusion' can be related in part to Žižek's example of how different approaches to the reading of a text exemplifies the triadic movement of positing, external and determinate reflection in Hegel.[20] (Žižek uses Sophocles' *Antigone* to make his point, but it holds just as well for *Oedipus*.) Positing reflection can be aligned with a hermeneutics of reading that claims access to the inner truth of a text: approaches couched in the language of certainty that allow for statements beginning '*Oedipus* is a play about . . .' (the tragedy of fate, the uncertainty of knowledge, the fragility of existence, tensions within fifth-century Athens and so on). External reflection is not so naïve as to fix on a true essence and acknowledges a plurality of readings that cannot be made to chime with one another. *Oedipus* has one meaning for the ancient Greeks, another meaning for Freud, still another one for existentialists and who knows what meanings in the future. Determinate reflection accepts the impossibility of ever recovering a putative essence and recognizes how the 'truth' of the text resides in these different readings. What matters is not to be found in what Sophocles might 'really' have been saying but in the subsequent interpretations that arise *afterwards* and the 'determinate reflection' is reached when we become aware of the fact that this delay is immanent, internal to the text itself. What to external reflection is a problem, the impossibility of ever arriving at a fixed interpretation, is paradoxically what constitutes the positive basis of what counts as truth: 'the Truth of a thing emerges because the thing is not accessible to us in its immediate self-identity'.[21] For Žižek, the way in which the fissure, the incompleteness, that creates the space for mutually exclusive readings is internal to the text is just one instance of what Hegelian philosophy is all about, namely that multiple determinations are necessary in order to embody the nullity in phenomena itself. This takes us well away from *Oedipus*, but what remains relevant in the notion of 'determinate reflection' is the idea that Sophocles' play is not to be studied in the vain hope of recovering what it is 'really about' because there is no such essence in the first place.

Empirical interpretations

Comparing Sophocles' drama to a detective story is not uncommon and as Oedipus goes about the task of tracking down the unknown assassin, or assassins, he proceeds like a professional detective: analysing evidence, looking for clues, issuing announcements, calling for public support, interviewing relevant individuals, summoning key witnesses, making deductions and drawing conclusions until a chief suspect is identified and brought to justice. The unexpected ending, for the detective at least, being the drawing around Oedipus of the hermeneutic circle.

Alerted by the oracle that Creon reported on, indicating that a clue is close at hand (111), Oedipus declares the need to find this clue and the chorus responds imaginatively to the call of the hunt:

> clearly the voice flashed forth,
> bidding each Theban track him down,
> the unknown murderer.
>
> (475–477)

The guilty man is on the run, the chorus proclaims, hiding in forests and caves (479–480). He will be found and hunted down.

The investigative drive of the judicious detective, the urge to track down clues and follow lines of evidence, also characterizes some intrepid interpreters of the drama who come up with their own pieces of puzzling evidence. When Creon reports on what he has heard from the oracle, he speaks at first of the need for 'banishing a man' (100), a single killer, but a few lines later he uses a plural, saying how the god commanded 'clearly' that 'some one punish with force this dead man's murderers' (107). Creon tells how the herdsman alleged a group of robbers were responsible (122) and this is what the chorus remembers hearing ('It was said that he was killed by certain wayfarers', 292). Oedipus speaks to Teiresias of

> an oracle declaring that our freedom
> from this disease would only come when we
> should learn the names of those who killed King Laius
> and kill them or expel from our country
>
> (304–309)

And Jocasta also speaks of a group of murderers (715–716) and how the whole city, not just herself, has always taken this to be the case. The herdsman comes under scrutiny as the sole survivor of the attack on Laius and the possibility exists, although this is never touched on by Sophocles, that he invented a plurality of killers to cover up for his cowardice in running away from the violent encounter with only one man; perhaps, too, when the herdsman returned to the city after the attack, he recognized the new king as the killer and begged to be allowed to leave Thebes for this reason (758ff.).

Voltaire, who wrote his own version of *Oedipus* and accompanied it with his 'Lettres sur Oedipe', is the first writer known to express surprise at the inconsistency in Sophocles' play over how many men killed Laius,[22] but the acme of empirically minded approaches to the play is reached when Oedipus is regarded as innocent of the crime or, at the very least, not convictable of the offence because the evidence against him is too weak and circumstantial. Thus Frederick Ahl, in his *Sophocles' Oedipus: Evidence & Self-Conviction*, argues that 'no conclusive evidence is presented that Oedipus killed his father and married his mother'.[23] Creon is accused of fabricating the 'evidence' of the oracle that he reports on at the start of the play, Teiresias is part of the conspiracy, and Oedipus convinces himself that he is indeed guilty. Readers too have been hoodwinked, bringing to the play a knowledge of the myth that clouds their judgement: 'what makes *Oedipus* perhaps the most astonishing of all Greek tragedies is its success in inducing readers to climb over all the obstacles . . . to share with Oedipus the conviction that he has 'proven himself to be the parricidal and incestuous child of Laios and Jocasta.'[24]

When Oedipus begins to suspect that he may be the killer, he calls for the sole witness to events at the crossroads to be brought to the city so that he can be cross-examined. He knows himself that he was alone when he killed strangers at the junction where three roads meet and if the witness confirms that a group of men killed Laius then his own innocence will be proved. Before this crucial matter can be clarified, the messenger from Corinth arrives and raises what for Oedipus is an even more crucial issue, that of his own parentage and identity. When the herdsman who is the witness finally arrives, he is called on to confirm what the messenger has reported about Oedipus' origins and the other matter is sidetracked and never resolved. This can seem odd because Sophocles could have cleared up this matter by having Oedipus ask the herdsman the relevant question, or having the answer emerge in the course of their conversation. The evidence that would condemn or clear Oedipus is never brought to light and so Oedipus may indeed be innocent of the crime of parricide. If this is the case, the theme of knowledge that runs through the drama – we don't know what we think we know – acquires an additional and startling dimension, never mind the more troubling implication this has for a reading of the play: 'To suggest that Oedipus may not have killed Laius is to play havoc with a legend that for twenty-eight hundred years has remained curiously intact.'[25]

An unsettling consequence and a possibly fatal weakness of an overly empirical approach to the play is that it can yield quite contradictory results, as can be seen in a plausible line of argument that builds on the reasonable assumption that·Oedipus is guilty of parricide and incest only to conclude that he knew this all along. This point of view, developed by Vellacott, sees Oedipus 'as having been aware of his true relationship to Laius and Jocasta ever since the time of his marriage' and only pretended to discover it many years later in the events enacted in the play.[26] The sleuth-like critic is again at work, asking questions and raising doubts, wondering if Oedipus could have arrived in Thebes two days after killing a stranger and not have connected the deed with the sudden slaying of the city's king. It seems inexplicable that Oedipus, renowned for his intelligence, could have been careless or reckless enough to have forgotten or ignored the oracle that prophecies he will kill his father and marry his mother, and marry a woman twice his age and kill a man old enough to be his father. Suspicion can arise from the way Oedipus slips into the singular when referring to the killing of Laius (138–140 even though Creon has just referred to the witness of the scene saying 'the robbers they encountered were many and the hands that did the murder were many' (122–123) and from the fact that Oedipus does not immediately summon this witness although it would be the logical thing to do. There are other pieces of the jigsaw that seem not to fit: the odd fact that when Oedipus came to Thebes and married Jocasta, he did not feel the need to ask about how her first husband died; along the same line, Jocasta seems to have no knowledge about the past life of her second husband (774ff.).

According to Vellacott, Oedipus knew the truth, but kept it hidden and acted the way he did in order to retain the trust of the Theban citizens, and he answers his rhetorical question: 'Was it difficult to get away with this story? We know that it was not; for we too have accepted it uncritically.'[27] Oedipus killed Laius when he lost his temper and married Jocasta in spite of the strong possibility that she was his mother. Many years later, understandably, he wants to preserve his secret. How could Oedipus live with such a secret? Vellacott thinks that 'Sophocles shows us in a number of passages the sort of defence-system which Oedipus has built for himself; a façade, a version of his story which made plausible sense and which he trained himself and others to accept.'

Approaches like this to *Oedipus* may remind some of A. C. Bradley's readings of Shakespeare, or rather L. C. Knights' famous rebuke to Bradley in his essay 'How Many Children had Lady Macbeth'.[28] What actually was wrote about Macbeth and children does not sound at all improper when compared to some of the speculations about *Oedipus*, but Bradley's remarks have come to be seen as emblematic of a critical approach that treats literary characters as if they were real people; however, as John Gould has pertinently observed:

> We may follow an everyday person home, but not a dramatic person. It is clearly not an *accident* that dramatic persons are only visible to us while on stage, nor can we even quite put it to ourselves like that. The spatial 'framing' of dramatic action is not a question of what is accessible, but of what exists: dramatic action *is* what we see (or are told of); we do not happen to see a part only of what exists.[29]

E. R. Dodds and John Gould

E. R. Dodds' 'On Misunderstanding the *Oedipus Rex*' was first published in 1966 and it remains a seminal essay on Sophocles' play, rejecting certain approaches to the drama in favour of an orientation that has been developed by John Gould in an equally important essay, 'The Language of *Oedipus*', first published twenty years later.

Dodds dismisses interpretations of the play that he regards as misleading, beginning with those who find in Aristotle's reference to *harmatia* grounds for thinking Oedipus must be guilty of a moral flaw. Dodds is also wary of approaches that step outside the boundaries of the play's action by treating it as a modern detective story: 'the *Oedipus Rex* is not a detective story but a dramatized folktale. If we insist on reading it as if it were a law report we must expect to miss the point.'[30] The point is also missed by reading the play in terms of free will and determinism: 'Certain of Oedipus' past actions were fate-bound; but everything that he does on the stage from first to last he does as a free agent.'[31] Misunderstandings arise from a Christian perspective that fails to acknowledge how early Greek thought did not feel the need to believe in divine justice. Oedipus is not guilty of murdering his father because there was no premeditation but this does not absolve him of the pollution that necessarily attaches itself to the act of killing one's father. This is what he accepts responsibility for and in doing so he rises above the level of ordinary humans, confronting and taking upon himself the accountability that comes from acts 'which are objectively most horrible' even though he himself is 'subjectively innocent'.[32]

Dodd's deservedly renowned essay is brief but decisive and it points to a metaphysical mystery about existence that lies at the heart of Sophocles' play. For Oedipus to be objectively guilty but subjectively innocent suggests an indeterminacy about being, about what used to be called the 'human condition', that does not allow for easy answers to questions concerning our place in the world and the sense we try to make of our lives. John Gould takes up and amplifies this theme, beginning his essay with lines from *King Lear*:

World, world, O world!
But that thy strange mutations make us hate thee,
Life would not yield to age.[33]

Mutability robs us of certainties and one way of accommodating the ontological insecurity that makes us all, as Dodds put it, 'grope in the dark as Oedipus gropes, not knowing who he is or what he has to suffer'[34] is to maintain an ironical distance from what may seem like reassuring truths or convictions. This is Gould's understanding of Sophoclean irony and he traces its course through the series of events making up the play and the studied ambivalence that attaches itself to key dramatic moments.

In the scene, for example, where an anxious Jocasta emerges from the palace and prays to Apollo for help with her distraught husband (911–923), a messenger from Corinth immediately appears with news of Polybus' death. It seems as if Apollo has answered her prayer and yet the messenger also brings information that will throw them into even deeper anxiety. The role of Apollo in all of this remains clouded in uncertainty, yet a troubling sense of some meaning behind the uncanny coincidences perturbs the audience.

Gould develops his concerns by first contrasting the secular language of Oedipus and Creon with the riddling discourse of Teiresias and then outlining the opposition between Thebes and Corinth as places of community, *poleis*, with an 'outer' space that lies beyond in the mountainsides and crossroads of Oedipus' other world. In his familiar world, Oedipus is a citizen and politician and this conditions his reaction to Teiresias' claim that he is the city's polluter and the killer of Laius. The prophet's wild claims only make sense to Oedipus, secular leader of Thebes, as evidence of a politically motivated plot. Creon also is politically minded and defends himself as such against the accusation that he is part of a conspiracy: 'He [Creon] and Oedipus speak the same language, a language which puts both beyond the range of understanding such as Teiresias' whose world is alien.'[35] Teiresias speaks in a different tongue, one that is opaque, eerie and teasing in its indeterminateness, and the tragic irony is not only that Oedipus is unable to respond to this register but that he is unaware of that aspect to his own nature that is equally strange and uncanny.

Oedipus' self-estrangement is bound up with an opposition between places that comes to the fore in the scene following Jocasta's intervention in the dispute between Creon and his brother-in-law (631–696). Her mention of a place where three roads meet takes us outside of Thebes and with Oedipus' realization that he may have killed the king comes the possibility that his curse divorces him from the place he calls home. In his cross-examination of the messenger and the herdsman there emerges an Oedipus who comes face to face with this other: a place outside of the *polis*, characterized by mountainside, caves and forests. The chorus, as if responding to this new dimension brought to the surface, imagines Oedipus as the child of a god and a mountain nymph and Cithaeron as his nursery:

> This is an image of his severance from human society, in which, despite his assurance of belonging, he has played parts that have mockingly inverted the most basic of human relationships, the most fundamental laws of social existence, in unawareness murdering his father and producing children by his own mother, to reduce the language of kinship to meaninglessness in becoming his children's brother and his mother's husband.[36]

The Oedipus who comes out from the palace at the end of the play is not the politically astute and socially aware citizen of Thebes who appeared from his palace at the start of the drama, and Gould shows how this makes itself felt in the language of the chorus. The chorus' unnerving response to Oedipus' curse on the man who rescued him from a certain infant death on the mountainside is to agree that it would have better had he never lived: 'I, too, could have wished it had been so' (1356).

Oedipus and the Real

Gould, delineating Oedipus' transition from a citizen of his community to a self-estranged isolate, speaks of his 'passage from the world of the falsely imagined to the world of the real'.[37] Consciously or not, Gould's reference to the 'real' evokes the psychoanalytic term employed by Lacan to refer to that which is not representable within the symbolic order. For Lacan, the Symbolic is a complex network of linguistic and cultural signs that bestows subjecthood, the chain of meaning whereby we make sense of the world and our position within it. The Real, on the other hand, functions as a limit, a negation, countering any construction within the Symbolic. The Real is not reality's ultimate referent but the gap, the void, around which the Symbolic is constructed. The Real is a consequence of an incompleteness in the ontological landscape and is associated with the traumatic nature of our entry into language and the abiding feeling that there is something missing in our own subjectivity, something strange and unbanishable at the heart of our identity which cannot be put into words. The proximity of the Real is an experience of discomfort, the feeling of being too close to something that cannot be understood, and the result can be a traumatic excess that threatens to engulf the symbolic realm and the security it provides by way of bestowing on us a sense of who we are.

Oedipus, in the course of an hour or so of his life, experiences the crumbling of the Symbolic order that gave meaning to his existence and in the process he comes to encounter the Real. He thought his place in the world was secure and consistent, that he could act with confidence and decisiveness as the ruler of Thebes and carer of his community, but events render him anchorless and alienated. He no longer belongs to human society, and the community of Thebans that is the chorus can no longer accommodate him. Oedipus encounters the Real and is lethally wounded because of what Heidegger called his 'passion for the unveiling of Being'.[38] His self-blinding is a wrecking of himself, the price paid for his insistence in wishing to know his identity.

The insight that Gould brings to *Oedipus* is to position the divine, the language of Apollo at Delphi and of Teiresias, outside of the Symbolic and close to the Real. This is the paradox and mystery of Apollo's presence in the drama: at one level, he is undeniably involved in what has happened, and yet at the same time he does not direct the human action, in just the way that the Lacanian Real is not itself an entity but a cause of which the effects appear in a displaced way. Oedipus passes beyond the world of symbolic meaning and confronts an aspect of existence, called the Thing by Lacan, that becomes an almost unbearable, visceral horror emanating from too close a proximity to the raw *being* and abyss of existence. Strip away the symbolic and vulnerable forms of identification that confer meaning on our sense of selfhood and what remains is an utter void, a remainder and a reminder of that which was never colonized by the symbolic order of language and culture, and this is what Oedipus experiences at the play's end:

> It is this sense of Oedipus' belonging not wholly among men but also to an alien world, outside our understanding, mocking the order, the rules, and values of human society, yet having its own coherence, its own logic of irony and coincidence – that is the central image of Sophocles' play. That other world is a world outside the limits of the human *polis*, penetrated

by the marginal, by shepherds and by seers. This, and not the driving force of fate not the issues of human or divine justice, is Sophocles' concern in *King Oedipus* and the true kernel of his religious statement.[39]

What Gould is remarking on here is a world that is not reducible to patterns of human intelligibility, a world that for Bernard Williams is also recognized by ancient Greeks as seemingly different as Thucydides and Sophocles: a 'sense of rationality at risk to chance' and an unwillingness to think we are safe in the belief that sense can be made of our human concerns.[40] One of the last thoughts expressed by Oedipus in the play is his conviction that he has become 'hateful to the gods' (*alla theois g'ekhthistos hēkō*, 1519), due presumably to his awful transgression. If this is the case and if the plague that ravaged Thebes was a manifestation of divine displeasure at what he had done, then it only intensifies the force of questioning why he, Oedipus should be singled out for something that happened to him accidentally. It is shock at the accidental nature of what has happened that for Oedipus is registered as the feeling of divine displeasure; fate is not a 'driving force' but the pitiless, inhuman necessity that emerges retrospectively when causes and consequences have been knitted together to provide a coherent account of how and why something happened in the way it did. Oedipus finds himself exposed to and powerless in the face of this necessity, a victim not of the gods, or his chromosomes or his culture, but of contingency: sheer bad luck. Sophocles' play shows that the Greeks were puzzled by aspects of human existence that have not been resolved in the two and a half millennia separating us from them.

Publishing history

The earliest known texts of Athenian tragedies like *Oedipus* date back to the fourth century, although none have survived, but written copies on papyrus would have been available from the late fifth century, by which time revivals of popular tragedies were taking place in Athens and possibly in smaller theatres in Attica as part of local festivals. Some at least were well known in Greek colonies in the south of Italy for after the failure of an Athenian expeditionary force to attack Syracuse in Sicily in 415 Athenian prisoners held captive there in stone quarries were said to have been reprieved in exchange for their recital of verses from the plays of Euripides. This suggests that revivals of popular plays were taking place in theatres outside of Attica, not only in Sicily but probably southern Italy and Macedon as well.

According to Plutarch, an Athenian law was introduced some time shortly after 340 calling for texts of tragedies by Sophocles (and Aeschylus and Euripides) to be kept for safe keeping by the state and used as the official basis for any future productions. By 300, Athenian dramas were performed in the theatres of most Greek cities and an indication of the popularity of *Oedipus* comes from a painting on a mixing bowl from Sicily, dated to the 330s, which is thought to depict a moment from Sophocles' play. The painting, apparently depicting the scene where Jocasta realizes the truth after the messenger from Corinth reveals how Oedipus was given to him by a herdsman working for Laius (924ff.), shows Jocasta half covering her face, raising her left hand to her cheek (a gesture of grief in Greek art), with Oedipus stroking his beard in puzzlement and the messenger looking straight ahead as if to an audience.[41]

There are no surviving accounts of critical responses to any of the tragedies until Aristotle set down some thoughts on the subject in the fourth century. His praise for *Oedipus*, regarding it as the exemplar of tragic drama, suggests it was well known at the time and this is backed up by a comic playwright, Antiphanes, remarking some hundred years after the first performance of Sophocles' play:

> Tragedy is a lucky kind of writing in every way. Its plots, in the first place, are well known to the audience before a line is spoken; all the poet need do is remind them. Suppose I just say 'Oedipus', they know the rest: father – Laius; mother – Jocasta; who his daughters and sons were; what it is that he did, and what he will suffer.[42]

In the city of Alexandria during the Hellenistic age, the period of ancient Greek history following the death of Alexander in 323, there began a tradition of critically commenting on literary texts stored at the city's great library. According to Galen (CE

129–199/217), the king of Egypt obtained the official texts of the plays of Sophocles, Aeschylus and Euripides from Athens upon payment of a large deposit of money and on the understanding that they would be returned after copying them, but he only returned the new copies and kept the originals for the city's library and its scholars.

Alexandrian scholars, then, had access to written texts on papyrus rolls of many Athenian dramas, including *Oedipus*, though whether these were originals from Athens or not cannot be known for sure. The scholars' cataloguing work led to commentaries as they sought to separate actors' interpolations from original text, offering philological and other information as well as critical comment of an ad hoc kind on tragedies that they considered worthy of such a degree of attention. Although there is much that is not known about how Alexandrian scholars went about their work, it was through their attention to particular texts than a canon began to emerge and Aristophanes of Byzantium (*c*.275–*c*.180), a Greek librarian at Alexandria from *c*.195, is thought to have been instrumental in setting up definitive texts for the plays of Sophocles, Aeschylus and Euripides. Throughout this Hellenistic period, revivals of these plays were also taking place throughout the Greek world, and fragments of papyri bearing lines from *Oedipus* and other tragedies have been found in the sands of Egypt. The largest source of such papyri are rubbish dumps south of modern Cairo at the ancient city of Oxyrhynchus and one part of *Papyrus Oxyrhynchus* (XVIII.2180), though not by any means the most important of the vast amount of papyrus texts uncovered, contains lines from *Oedipus* that modern scholars have found useful in clarifying some textual uncertainties.

More important for the survival and transmission of *Oedipus* and the other ancient tragedies that have come down to us was the influence of this literature on Roman culture, beginning in the early decades of the third century BCE, long before a decisive Roman military victory over the Greeks in 146. Some acquaintance, if not knowledge, of Greek tragedy became a conventional aspect of the education of the Roman elite; as a young man Julius Caesar is said to have written a version of *Oedipus*[43] and, more significantly, Seneca (*c*.1 BCE–CE65) wrote a hugely influential version of the same Greek tragedy (see page 126). Some time early in the third century CE there emerged an agreement that a selection of plays, seven each by Sophocles (including *Oedipus*) and Aeschylus and ten by Euripides, were especially worthy of study, and in this way the other plays began gradually to go out of circulation. Two developments in the media for preserving written texts helped ensure the survival of the twenty four plays that had emerged as the canon of Athenian tragedy. First came the codex, replacing the scrolls of papyrus by their collection into sheets which were fastened together at the spine and capable of being protected by a cover made of wood; then came the use of parchment by means of treating the skin of sheep, goats and calves to make a material for writing which was far more durable than papyrus.

While libraries in Rome were destroyed following incursions by Goths and Vandals in the fifth century, those in Byzantium, capitol of the eastern half of the former Roman empire, survived and continued to preserve copies of *Oedipus* and other Athenian tragedies even though nothing is known about their existence from the sixth to the ninth centuries. While knowledge of Greek became close to extinct in what had been the western part of the Roman empire, and remained so until Constantinople (Byzantium) was captured by the Ottomans in 1453, codices which included *Oedipus* gathered dust in Byzantium, monasteries and in some eastern church libraries. Around the middle of the ninth century, a cultural renewal led to monastic scribes making manuscript copies of pagan literature, probably funded by wealthy patrons, and the following century saw the compilation of the *Suda*, a huge Byzantine encyclopaedia written in Greek with thousands of entries that would have drawn on ancient sources. The *Suda* includes biographical information on Sophocles as well as containing over a hundred entries relating to *Oedipus*.[44]

The earliest surviving copy of *Oedipus*, written on vellum in a scriptorium in Byzantium in the second half of the tenth century or early eleventh, is part of a manuscript known as *Mediceus Laurentianus 32.9*.[45] It was brought to Italy around 1423, at a time of renewed interest in Hellenism in that country, and became part of the private library of Niccolò Niccoli (it is now in the Laurentian Library in Florence). It had been tracked down in Constantinople by Giovanni Aurispa, a savant who had learned Greek on the island of Chios and where ten years earlier he had found a manuscript that also contained a copy of *Oedipus* and which was also sold to Niccolò Niccoli.

There is a twin manuscript, now in Leiden, of the mid-tenth-century one but it is a palimpsest and largely unreadable. The second-oldest surviving copy of *Oedipus* was written in the second half of the twelfth century and is known as Laurentianus 31.10. Other medieval manuscripts of the play dating from between the thirteenth and fifteenth centuries are now housed in the Nazionale Marciana in Venice, the Vatican, the Bibliothèque Nationale in Paris and the university libraries of Oxford and Cambridge. Probably beginning some time in the first half of the sixteenth century, a small number of manuscripts of Greek tragedies began to be purchased by university libraries outside of Italy; and when printed copies became available, *Oedipus* soon reached other parts of western Europe and a far wider audience.

At the end of the fifteenth century Aldus Manutius established his Aldine printing press in Venice and he was the first to print *Oedipus*, as part of a 1502 edition of the plays of Sophocles (in Greek). By the time of Thomas Moore's fictional *Utopia*, published fourteen years later, the traveller Raphael Hythloday packed an Aldine copy of Sophocles when he made his fourth voyage to the island.[46] *Oedipus* became the Greek tragedy *par excellence* during the Renaissance, a legacy of the status Aristotle had accorded it in his *Poetics*, although what chiefly motivated Renaissance intellectuals was a desire to trace the influence of Greek culture on Latin literature. This was their primary interest and in 1558 the first Latin translation of *Oedipus* was published in Paris.

Testimony to the canonical status of *Oedipus* came in 1585 when the first public performance of the play since ancient times took place in Vicenza (and it remained the only professional production for another two hundred years) to mark the opening of the Teatro Olimpico, designed by Palladio. Now the world's oldest surviving enclosed theatre, the interior scenery was designed by another Venetian architect, Scamozzi, who took over after the death of Palladio and his stage set, which has somehow survived the centuries and can still be seen, is a remarkable trompe-lœil representing the (Palladian) streets of ancient Thebes. The choice of *Oedipus* for the theatre's opening is testimony to its pre-eminence at the time and it was translated into Italian for the occasion.

A notable French translation of *Oedipus*, by André Dacier, was published in 1692 and an influential English translation by Thomas Francklin appeared in 1754 (the first full but less than mellifluous translation into English, by George Adams, had appeared twenty five years earlier). Hölderlin's powerful German translation was published in 1804. Sophocles was very popular in Germany and Britain throughout the nineteenth century – George Eliot put him on the same level as Shakespeare and told the classical scholar R. C. Jebb that Sophocles had influenced her 'in the delineation of the great primitive emotions'[47] – but the subject matter of *Oedipus* did not go down well with the Christian Establishment and it was barred from the English stage between 1886 and 1912 on the grounds of public decency.

Textual criticism of *Oedipus* had begun with the anonymous scholiasts in Alexandria and given the likelihood that the number of textual errors increased each time a copy was made of an existing manuscript, there was a pressing need for scholarly attention to be devoted to the editions that began to be published in print from the Renaissance onwards. Such work got underway as early as the middle of the sixteenth century when an Italian scholar, Victorius, consulted different manuscripts of *Oedipus* before publishing a new edition, but it reached its acme in Germany in the nineteenth century. German scholars restituted with a passion the work that had begun in Hellenistic times and the endeavour to annotate and emend classical texts became the hallmark of their country's scholarship. What tended to be ignored in this highly specialized tradition of exhaustive inquiry into grammatical and semantic cruces and conjectures was an aesthetically more appreciative response to a Greek text as a work of literature, one that was respected but went beyond pure linguistic analysis and hair-splitting philological distinctions. Such a response was achieved by the British scholar R. C. Jebb (1841–1905) and his 1893 edition of *Oedipus*, part of a seven-volume edition of the plays of Sophocles published between 1883 and 1896, still stands as one of the finest translations of the play. Its value was quickly recognized and more than one generation of English-speakers became acquainted with Sophocles' play through Jebb because his translation was widely used, minus the Greek text, introduction and commentaries, in anthologies of Greek literature. It was republished in 2004 with his introduction, facing pages of the Greek text and his English prose translation and his commentary in double columns below. An outstanding virtue of Jebb's translation, valuable for readers with or without some knowledge of the original language, is its reproduction of the order of the Greek clauses and its meticulous attention to the use of Greek particles. When it comes to learned discussions of philological matters, Jebb declares his self-restraint in reporting 'only those readings of MSs which have a direct critical interest' and omitting material which would only interest the 'palaeograpical student'.[48]

When W. B. Yeats was looking for a translator of the play (see page 137), he first asked the classicist Gilbert Murray, but early in 1905 the invitation was declined in a letter which also expressed Murray's feelings about the play:

> Sophocles no doubt did many bad things in his life; I would not try to shield him from just blame. But in this case I am sure he is in a trance and his body was possessed by a series of devils . . . I rather hope you won't do the Oedipus. It is not the play for you to cast your lot with.[49]

Murray had already achieved fame for his translations of Euripides in rhyming couplets and eventually overcame his objections to Sophocles' play and his version of Oedipus was published in 1911 and reprinted many times in the years that followed.[50] It proved to be as influential as his work on Euripides, introducing Sophocles to a very large audience of readers in the 1920s and 1930s. When in 1912 Oedipus was produced for the first time on a London stage, directed by Max Reinhardt and using Murray's translation, it was a tremendous success and enhanced the appeal of Murray's translation. Reinhardt had first achieved success with Oedipus in Berlin, using a translation by Hugo van Hofmannshtal, and it had been performed in most European capitals before Reinhardt planned a production in English.

Reinhardt was a famous German director and, before using Murray's English translation, his production of Oedipus had already achieved fame after its first staging in Germany two years earlier. Influenced by German archaeological work into the Greek theatre, he had sought to recreate for his audiences aspects of the theatrical experience that Athenians once enjoyed. Since then his production had travelled across Europe and for its appearance in Britain he had the theatre in Covent Garden altered to suit his requirements; his original intention had been to use the Albert Hall because of its shape and grand size. In a way that departed radically from the conventions of the time, the front rows of stalls were removed and the proscenium stage and the orchestral pit changed in order to bring the audience closer to the actors (who made their entrances and exits through the audience). The effect was to introduce a new form of theatre to British audiences and a fresh appreciation of Sophocles' play:

> Perhaps the most artistic effect was that attained by the crowd and Oedipus. Oedipus stood on the rostrum calm and self-possessed. Beneath him surged the infuriated mob, with outstretched arms, swelling up to him like a sea of angry emotions, and returning thence to the Leader of the Chorus in response to his call. There on one side Oedipus stood like an intellectual pinnacle islanded in the billowing ocean of human beings; and there on the other side the Leader stood like the Spirit of the Infinite swayed to and fro by elemental passions.[51]

Gilbert Murray was delighted by what he saw and praised it in *The Times*: 'The half-naked torchbearers with loin-cloths and long black hair made my heart leap with joy. There was real early Greece about them, not the Greece of the schoolroom or the conventional art studio.'[52] Nor, though, was it the Greece of Sophocles.[53]

Since the times of Jebb and Murray, there have been a number of editions of *Oedipus* in Greek and numerous translations (see page 157). More of a translation than an adaptation, Anthony Burgess' *Sophocles Oedipus the King* acknowledges itself as both, a rare hybrid in which 'nothing that he [Sophocles] wrote has been taken away, but something has been added.'[54] What accounts for the additional material is the fascination Burgess brings to the Sphinx's involvement with Oedipus and what this reveals about a relationship between riddles and incest. Burgess finds in Lévi-Strauss evidence of such a linkage in primitive societies where the dangerous threat of incest is embodied in the mystery of the chimerical riddler, a confrontation with whom must be avoided at any cost. The Sphinx as both animal and human is a monstrous deviation from the allowed course of nature and her substance becomes the taboo that must be observed. For Burgess, this explains an undeniably odd aspect to the Greek myth: why did the Sphinx's simple riddle remain unanswered for so long, especially in view of the fatal consequence for those who failed what was hardly a brainteaser? His answer is that the riddle was there to be avoided, not answered, for giving the solution to the puzzle was more dangerous than not answering it. The riddle is the knot which gives stability to the social order and untying it threatens the survival of the *polis*. The ease of answering the riddle is akin to the ever-present possibility of committing incest and must be continually resisted. The play shows how Oedipus is 'the cause of the state's disease and disruption but also, through his discovery of and expiation for sin, the cause of its recovered health. He is a criminal but also a saint. In other words he is a tragic hero.'[55]

Burgess' *Oedipus* was first published in 1972 and in his later novel, *Earthly Powers*, the character Kenneth Toomey is a playwright and he has his own version of Sophocles' play, 'more of an adaptation than a translation' according to Toomey, and lines from it are quoted when his brother-in-law, having discovered he is illegitimate and knows not the identity of his father, recalls them as appropriate to his situation. The lines are not part of Burgess' *Oedipus*:

I must unlock this last door to the last room
Where I myself am lodged. I must look on myself.
At worst, I am the son of the goddess Fortune.
Who would not have such a mother? I am
Kin to the seasons – four-legged spring,
Summer upright in his pride, tottering winter.
I rise and fall and rise and fall with the
Rising and falling year. This is my breed.
I ask no other.[56]

Notes

1 Philocles is only mentioned by name in one medieval manuscripts.

2 Burian (2009), p. 101; Macintosh (2009), p. 5.

3 Segal (1983), p. 76.

4 Jones (1980), p. 13.

5 Aristotle (1996), p. 12.

6 'The question asked is this: if insulted and assaulted by someone travelling in the opposite direction from you, is killing him the mark of a feisty Bronze Age hero defending his dignity, or of a dangerously violent, even psychotic individual?' Hall (2010), p. 302.

7 Knox (1983), p. 5.

8 Segal (1999), p. 232.

9 Ibid., p. 242.

10 The idea that there is something uplifting or profoundly, if mysteriously, ennobling about the suffering endured by the central character in a tragedy is effectively debunked in a chapter in Terry Eagleton's (2003) *Sweet Violence: The Idea of the Tragic* ('The Value of Agony').

11 The looking for and finding of ritual elements in Greek tragedy does not win favour with Oliver Taplin and he dismisses applying ideas of a 'yearly spirit' to the genre: 'But not one single tragedy we have can be claimed without distortion actually to follow this pattern; in particular Greek tragedy does not go in for resurrection or rejuvenation.' Taplin (1983), p. 3.

12 Fergusson (1949); Vernant (1983).

13 Fergusson (1949), p. 59.

14 Vernant (1983), p. 198.

15 Vernant (1983), p. 208.

16 Burian (2009), p. 103.

17 'His resurgence in the last scene of the play is a prophetic vision of a defeated Athens which will rise to a greatness beyond anything she had attained in victory, a vision of man, superior to the tragic reversal of his action and the terrible success of his search for truth, reasserting his greatness, not this time in defiance of the powers which shape human life but in harmony with those powers'. Knox (1957), p. 266.

18 Burian (2009), p. 115.

19 Sommerstein (2010), p. 223.

20 Žižek (1989), pp. 213–214.

21 Ibid., p. 214.

22 Voltaire (1877), pp. 1–58.

23   Ahl (1991), p. x.

24   Ibid., p. 264.

25   Goodhart (1978), p. 61.

26   Vellacott (1971), p. 104. Vellacott estimates Oedipus' age as eighteen or nineteen when he killed Laius and thirty six at the time of the play's opening scene (p. 107).

27   Vellacott (1971), p. 119.

28   Bradley (1941), pp. 488–492; Knights (1979).

29   Gould (2001), p. 80.

30   Dodds (1968), p. 21.

31   Ibid., pp. 22–23.

32   Ibid., p. 28.

33   Quoted from Gould (2001), p. 244.

34   Dodds (1968), p. 28.

35   Gould (2001), p. 252.

36   Ibid., p. 258.

37   Ibid.

38   Ibid.

39   Gould (2001), p. 262.

40   Williams (1994), p. 164.

41   There are also two other female figures in the painting, taken to be the two daughters of Oedipus and Jocasta who appear at the end of the play but not in this scene. The painting, then, is not a precise depiction of a scene from the play. See Taplin (1997), pp. 84–88.

42   Quoted in Easterling and Knox (2003), p. 412.

43   Suetonius, *Divus Julius*, 56.7, www.perseus.tufts.edu/hopper/text?doc=Perseus:text:1999.02.0061 (accessed 1 October 2011).

44   www.stoa.org/sol (accessed 1 October 2011).

45   'It forms a volume measuring 12¼ by 8½ inches, and containing 264 leaves (= 528 pages), of which Sophocles fills 118 leaves (= 236 pages).' Jebb (2004), p. iiii.

46   Moore, Thomas. *Utopia*. Great Literature Online. 1997–2011.http://moore.classicauthors.net/Utopia/Utopia5.html (accessed 1 October 2011).

47   Quoted in Sophocles, Meineck and Woodruff (2003), p. xxxv.

48   Jebb (2004), p. lvii.

49   Quoted in Clark and McGuire (1989), p.9.

50   www.gutenberg.org/files/27673/27673-h/27673-h.htm (accessed 1 October 2011).

51   Carter (1964), pp. 218–219 (available online at www.archive.org, accessed 1 October 2011).

52   Ibid., pp. 221–222.

53   Arnott (1959), p. 220: 'Of this exciting spectacle one can only say that it was magnificent, but it was not Sophocles'.

54   Burgess (2001), p.4.

55   Ibid., p. 6.

56   Burgess (1981), p. 390.

CHAPTER SIX

Adaptation, interpretation and influence

In an essay by Herder on Shakespeare, published in 1773, French neoclassical dramatists are criticized for their slavish adherence to Aristotle's account of Greek tragedy.[1] The mistake they make, according to Herder, is to take an artistic form that belongs to a particular historical moment and elevate it into a universal and prescriptive standard. In so doing, they ignore the fact that the art specific to a historical period cannot simply be transposed into another age, like that of seventeenth-century France, without losing what is intrinsically meaningful about the art of a previous age. Shakespeare is seen not to have made this mistake and, paradoxically, remains closer to the spirit of the Greeks by departing from Aristotelian 'unities' of time, place and action and giving expression to what was meaningful in his own age. When it comes to adaptations and translations of *Oedipus*, Herder's distinction can be adapted to signal a basic division between those that in varying degrees of self-awareness retain a fidelity to the Greek experience of life as expressed in the Athenian theatre of the fifth century, and those that depart from that ground but use the Greek material to give expression to a different view of the world. In this sense, Herder does highlight an important hermeneutical issue that arises when considering the very different kinds of adaptations and translations of Sophocles' play.

Seneca and Ted Hughes

The influence of Athenian tragedy upon Roman culture was profound and can be traced back to the performances in the theatres of Greek colonies in Sicily and southern Italy. Seneca's tragedies, the only surviving examples of Roman tragedy, include a version of the Oedipus story and from before the Renaissance until the end of the eighteenth century Seneca's *Oedipus* was more influential than the play by Sophocles on which it is closely based.[2]

Seneca's drama opens with a guilt-ridden Oedipus, haunted by the prophecy which drove him from Corinth and the conviction that his own 'touch of death' has brought the plague to Thebes: 'Can death still be denied, although so near, to me alone?'[3] There are graphic descriptions of the devastation wrought by the plague and, a ritual sacrifice been ordered by Teiresias, a graphically gory description by the prophet's daughter of the animals' entrails. Teiresias, perturbed by what he hears, requests that the ghost of Laius be summoned, leading to another vivid narrative when Creon describes how he carried out this task. Sophocles' plotline is now followed fairly closely, with Oedipus accusing his brother-in-law of conspiracy to dethrone him, a Corinthian messenger arriving with news of Polybus' death and the revelation about Oedipus' origins. The herdsman is questioned, the truth emerges and a messenger describes in gruesome detail Oedipus' self-blinding. Departing from Sophocles, Seneca keeps Jocasta alive until after this deed and she kills herself in front of Oedipus, who addresses her as his mother, after blaming Fate for their tragedy. Oedipus concurs but finds some relief as the scapegoat:

> I shall take away
> All the infections of mortality
> That have consumed this land. Come deadly Fates
> Come, all grim spectre of Disease, black Plague,

Corruption and intolerable Pain!
Come with me! I could want no better guides.[4]

T. S. Eliot could appreciate Seneca's dramatic power but he identifies an oratorical aspect to his art that serves to limit the Roman playwright:

> Behind the dialogue of Greek drama we are always conscious of a concrete visual actuality, and behind that of a specific emotional actuality . . . In the plays of Seneca, the drama is all in the word, and the word has no further reality behind it.[5]

This is an unforgiving judgement but is representative of the modern tendency to denigrate Seneca's dramaturgy, regarding it as a travesty of what the Greeks achieved, without considering the differences in form and content and the inescapable fact that readers (audiences are rarer because Seneca is so infrequently performed) invariably come to it in the wake of some knowledge of Sophocles' original. Consequently, a production of Seneca's play requires innovation on the part of an adventurous director to give aesthetic justice to the dream-like quality that pervades its doom-laden, deterministic universe.[6] T. S. Eliot's Christian faith in the possibility of redemption made it difficult for him to respond to this, whereas Ted Hughes, who made his own translation and version of Seneca's *Oedipus*, was able to do so. His *Oedipus*, successfully used in stage productions of the play, beginning in 1968 at the Old Vic Theatre in London under the direction of Peter Brooks and with John Gielgud as Oedipus, gave voice to his conviction that Seneca was able to articulate a raw and blunt paganism discernible in Sophocles:

> The Greek world saturates Sophocles too thoroughly: the evolution of his play seems complete, fully explored and in spite of its blood-roots, fully civilized. The figures in Seneca's *Oedipus* are Greek only by convention: by nature they are more primitive than aboriginals.[7]

Hughes worked from a nineteenth-century translation of Seneca's *Oedipus*, subtracting the ornate Victorian language, paring it down to the kernel of meaning as he saw it. The final result bears little relation to the language of Seneca, as in the opening speech by Oedipus:

> I stand in it [fear] like a blind man in darkness even now what is fate preparing for me surely I see that how could I be mistaken this plague slaughtering everything that lives no matter what men trees flies no matter it spares me why what final disaster is it saving me for the whole nation guttering the last dregs of its life no order left ugly horrible deaths in every doorway every path wherever you look funeral after funeral endless terror and sobbing and in the middle of it all I stand here untouched the man marked down by the god for the worst fate of all a man hated and accused by the god still unsentenced.[8]

Oedipus also figures in *Crow*, a collection of poems Hughes was writing around the same time he was working on his version of Seneca's *Oedipus*. In 'Song for a Phallus' Oedipus kills his mother and the Sphinx with an axe and although the tone is mocking, with its nursery-rhyme cadence and satirical use of Freud, there is a sense of something deeply misogynistic and repressive about the poem that may have more to do with the poet's inner demons than anything to be found in Sophocles or Seneca. When Oedipus kills the Sphinx in Hughes' poem 'out there came ten thousand ghosts' crying he will 'never know / What a cruel bastard God is'. Oedipus then 'stabs his Mammy in the guts / And smiles into her face':

> He split his Mammy like a melon
> He was drenched with gore
> He found himself curled up inside
> As if he had never been bore
> Mamma Mamma[9]

Corneille, Dryden and Voltaire

The concerns and dramatic renditions of three neoclassical adaptations of *Oedipus*, dating from the mid-seventeenth century to the early eighteenth century, depart as obviously from Sophocles as they do from the interests of modern audiences, something reflected in the fact that they are rarely if ever revived for the stage or translated into English.

Corneille's *Oedipe* was published in 1659 becoming such a success on the stage of the Comédie-Française when it opened in 1680 that it was still part of the theatre's repertoire in 1729. At first, the play has little in common with its ancient Greek ancestor, with Corneille adding a political love story to the plot involving Thésée (Theseus, the king of Athens) and Dircé, a daughter from the marriage of Jocasta and Laius. Oedipus opposes the prospect of the lovers' marriage out of fear that, as the natural heir to the throne of Thebes, Dircé would be a threat to his rule were she to marry a king like Thésée. There is a change of direction in the last third of the play when an Oedipus that we can recognize from Sophocles emerges after the ghost of Laius demands atonement for his death. The truth comes to light and Oedipus accepts his fate and blinds himself, attaining the status of a tragic if haughty hero. Redemption comes in the form of a miraculous lifting of the plague and Oedipus' self-punishment is seen to achieve closure vis-à-vis his father: '*Le sang de Laius a rempli son devoir, / Son Ombre est satisfaite*', says Theseus, the lover of Dircé at the end of the drama.[10]

Twenty years after Corneille's *Oedipe*, John Dryden and Nathaniel Lee wrote their own version of Sophocles' play and it became as popular in England as Corneille's play had been in France and remained as successful on the stage for just as long. The exact division of labour between Dryden and Lee is not known, but Dryden wrote most of it. As was the case in France, the need for additional material was felt to be necessary for a successful production of the drama and Dryden copied Corneille's idea of a love-based subplot. This time it is Eurydice, daughter of Laius and the step-daughter of Oedipus, and she falls in love with Adrastus, the king of Argos. The subplot becomes more elaborate when a villainous, hunchbacked Creon desires Eurydice for himself and this leads to him killing her and then dying in a fight with Adrastus (who also dies). The Jacobean-style bloodbath is completed when Jocasta kills herself and her children, and Oedipus throws himself from Thebes' palace walls. A prurient eroticism adds some spice to what is more a case of melodrama than a tragic downfall and the play as a whole, despite Dryden's professed admiration for Sophocles, bears witness more to Seneca and Corneille than to the Athenian drama.

Voltaire's *Oedipe*, written in 1817 when he was in prison, was the first play he wrote and, as noted already, in the 'Lettres sur Oedipe' he expresses his incredulity at some aspects of the plot.[11] He finds it difficult to accept that nearly twenty years could have passed between the killing of Laius and an investigation to establish who was the assailant. In Voltaire's adaptation the intervening period of time is reduced to four years and this includes a two-year period between the killing and the arrival of Oedipus in Thebes. In a similar spirit of rationalization, Voltaire's Oedipus is portrayed as an enlightened ruler who speedily and judiciously makes sense of the clues and realizes that he is the parricide; the discovery of his incest comes later and as part of the unfolding drama it is underplayed. A romantic subplot is introduced when Philoctetes, who has always loved Jocasta, turns up in Thebes and is accused by citizens of having murdered Laius. This though leads nowhere, becoming merely an interlude and unlike the subplots of Corneille and Dryden is not integrated into the main drama. The play comes to an end with Jocasta stabbing herself after Oedipus' self-blinding.

One critic, responding to the adaptations of Corneille, Dryden and Voltaire, asks what it is that makes them seem qualitatively inferior to Sophocles' drama:

> It is not that they are derivative, but that they are in some sense reductive, that they offer to explain in terms of will or passion or morality what in Sophocles exists prior to rationalisation and remains finally immune to explanation.[12]

Hölderlin, Nietzsche and Heidegger

Hölderlin completed his translation into German in 1802 and worked on it again before it was published two years later; an English translation by David Constantine was published in 2001, ten years after Hölderlin's version had appeared in Italian and three years after a French translation. Hölderlin's translation and its availability in three other languages together make up the most poetic versions of Sophocles' play available and it is difficult to imagine them being bettered in this respect. The German text was greeted with consternation by critics after its publication, alarmed by what they saw as a travesty of the German language and unable to comprehend why anyone would want to push language beyond what they saw as its limits (it was 1921 before a stage version was produced). This straining of language as Hölderlin strives to recreate the syntax of the Greek and the literal makeup of some individual words is the very quality that makes his version so luminous and, fortunately, Constantine manages to recreate it in his English version.

Hölderlin was not a scholar of the Greek language and his translation contains hundreds of philological errors, many of which may be due to his use of a Greek text from the middle of the sixteenth century, but it stands as a courageous, affecting and accurate version of what the critic above finds missing from Corneille, Dryden and Voltaire, something 'prior to rationalization' in one sense but not immune to expression in poetry. In the scene between Oedipus and Teiresias, for example, there are seven lines which Jebb translates fairly literally but not without distinction:

> And what place shall not be harbour to thy shriek, what of all Cithaeron shall not ring with it soon, when thou has learnt the meaning of the nuptials in which, within that house, thou didst find a fatal haven, after a voyage so fair? And a throng of other ills thou guessest not, which shall make thee level with thy true self and with thine own breed.
>
> (419–425)

Hölderlin uses the same number of lines as Jebb, remaining surprisingly faithful to the Greek while also conveying a poetic force of his own that condenses itself into the sparse, troubling summation of 'It has no shore':

> And of your screams what harbour will not be
> Full and what Cithaeron soon not shout with you?
> Do you feel the marriage as you landed
> Voyaging well? It has no shore. Not of
> The other evils either do you feel the host
> That strikes you with your children equally.[13]

Hölderlin also wrote some notes on *Oedipus* which are remarkably recondite but nonetheless intriguing. He speaks of tragedy as attending to the singularity of things 'in the medium of its appearance' and how this requires a 'caesura', a disruption that directs attention to the finitude of things, which he identifies in Sophocles' play as occurring in the encounter of Oedipus with Teiresias. He thinks Oedipus reacts too quickly to Creon's report and, instead of waiting for the priest to arrive and conduct appropriate purification rites, insists on questioning Creon further and thereby triggering an investigation that was not strictly necessary. Hölderlin sees Oedipus as usurping the role of the priest by responding 'too infinitely' to the oracle that Creon reports, adopting it as a divine command, forcing himself into an illicit realm through the force of his will and a demand for an unlimited clarity that is appropriate only to the gods. He wants to 'integrate his present reality and the unfolding future with his hidden beginnings' and thereby attain a state of knowledge that would transcend his individuality.[14] Oedipus' *jouissance* only comes to an end when his transgression takes him beyond the human and into an order that belongs more properly to the divine, what Hölderlin calls the 'zone of the dead'. To attempt such a fusion paradoxically creates the 'separation' that defines tragedy, a dialectical split between unformed nature and consciousness:

> Tragedy consists chiefly in this: that the monstrousness of the pairing of God and Man and the boundless coming together in anger of the powers of Nature and the innermost heart of man, is grasped in the catharsis of that boundless union through boundless separation.[15]

The highly condensed style of writing here makes it difficult to follow what Hölderlin is saying, but talk of a coupling that brings disjunction is part of his view of Oedipus as someone who asserts himself to excess and whose frenzied spirit drives him to fulfil the oracle's call to make good the spilt blood of Laius. What he calls the 'innermost heart of man' is revealed when Oedipus is warned by Jocasta to desist – 'If you're chary of life / Then do not search' – and he stands uncowed:

> Let break what must. I want my kith and kin
> However base, I want to learn it . . .

Small and large
The moons born at my time surrounded me
And so produced I will not exit so
But will discover wholly what I am.[16]

In his notes, Hölderlin comments on these lines spoken by Oedipus in order to explain how his restless curiosity insists on asserting itself until finally the 'boundless separation' between his urgent intellectualism and facts overwhelms him:

And precisely this questing after everything, this interpreting of everything, is the reason why in the end his spirit is defeated by the rough and simple language of his servants.[17]

This idea of an excessive searching for knowledge that can only result in tragedy accords with lines from a prose poem, known by the beginning of its first line as 'In Lovely Blueness' ('In lieblicher Bläue'), which is attributed to Hölderlin though his authorship is not certain: 'man has eyes, as opposed to the moon, which has light. King Oedipus has an eye too many perhaps. The sufferings of this man, they seem indescribable, unspeakable, inexpressible.'[18]

Nietzsche read Hölderlin with admiration and respect and his own view of Greek tragedy and *Oedipus* in particular helps in understanding what Hölderlin was struggling to express in his notes about Sophocles' drama. As professor of Greek at the University of Basle, where he worked for ten years, Nietzsche taught Greek tragedy and a number of his handwritten outlines for lectures have survived. They show how he introduced what he saw as a duality in Greek thought between what he called the Apollonian, representing order and self-control, and a contrary impulse towards excess and dissolution that he termed Dionysian. This idea was developed in *Birth of Tragedy*, an intellectual tour de force which was published in 1872 and caused tremendous consternation in an academic community highly unreceptive to Nietzsche's iconoclastic ideas.

Nietzsche is drawn to Sophocles' Oedipus as a figure of undeserved suffering, a man who 'does not sin'.[19] He writes of Oedipus as someone who encounters the Real when he unwittingly enters forbidden territory: 'for how could nature be forced to give up its secrets otherwise than by a triumphant violation, that is through the unnatural? . . . he who plunges nature into the abyss of annihilation must experience the dissolution of nature as it affects him personally'.[20] This is the foundation for Dionysian wisdom, an insight into the abyss of life's meaninglessness, and the pessimism it entails is rendered bearable because Sophoclean tragedy also embraced an Apollonian aesthetic that enshrined respect for a world of phenomena and illusion that sustained a belief in self-affirmation. Oedipus, 'the most painful figure of the Greek stage', embodies this unique blend of the Dionysian and Apollonian:

> If, after a powerful attempt to stare at the sun, we turn away blinded with dark spots before our eyes, as a remedy so to speak, then the projected images of the Sophoclean hero are the opposite of this – in short, the Apollonian qualities of the mask are the necessary results of a glance into the terrifying inner world of nature, bright spots so to speak to heal the eyes which have been damaged by the sight of the terrible darkness.[21]

Heidegger also brings a metaphysical weight to Athenian tragedy and in a way that is not greatly dissimilar to Nietzsche, although he expresses this in the terms of his own philosophy. He refers approvingly to Hölderlin's line 'King Oedipus has an eye too many perhaps' in his *Introduction to Metaphysics*, written in the mid-1930s. Heidegger views the achievement of ancient Greek tragedy in terms of a revealing of being and he writes of Oedipus being hurled out of a 'seeming':

> This seeming is not just Oedipus' subjective view of himself, but that within which the appearing of his Dasein [being] happens. In the end, he is unconcealed in his Being as the murderer of his father and the defiler of his mother . . . Oedipus goes to unveil what is concealed. In doing so, he must, step by step, place himself into an unconcealment that in the end he can endure only by gouging out his own eyes.[22]

Oedipus, for Heidegger, exemplifies 'the passion for the unveiling of Being' and this is how he understands the line from Hölderlin's poem: 'This eye too many is the fundamental condition for all great questioning and knowing as well as their sole metaphysical ground. The knowledge and science of the Greeks are this passion'.[23]

Psychoanalysis and *Oedipus*

A production of *Oedipus* that started in 1881 at the Comédie-Française in Paris, the theatre where Corneille's and Voltaire's versions had been performed, used a verse translation in rhyming couplets that had been published nearly thirty years earlier, and the leading part was played by Jean Mounet-Sully, already one of the best actors in France. Mounet-Sully's reputation soared even higher as a result of his performances as Oedipus, helping to make the production a success across Europe.[24] One of those who saw this production, Sigmund Freud, had first read Sophocles' play in 1873 and according to his biographer, the performance 'made a deep impression on him'.[25]

Freud's Oedipus is libidinally innocent and when he writes in *Interpreting Dreams* about the desire to kill one's father and sleep with one's mother he refers to Sophocles' play and does not offer a psychoanalytic account of Oedipus. *Oedipus*, he explains, is commonly understood as a tragedy about fate, the inexorability of divine will versus the futile endeavours of humans to resist it, but this cannot be the source of the play's fascination because other playwrights have composed stories around the same theme without touching a raw nerve in the way *Oedipus* does:

The only reason why his fate grips us is because it might also have been our own, because prior to our birth the oracle uttered the same curse over us as over him. It was given to us all, possibly, to direct our first sexual stirring at our mother, our first hatred and violent wish at our father; our dreams persuade us of that.[26]

According to Freud, Sophocles' play moves us because we are the desiring subject – Freud recalls Jocasta telling Oedipus, in an attempt to ease his fear over the possibility of having sex with his mother, that it is not uncommon for a man to dream of such an act (981–984) – and the play's (male) audience has little choice but to acknowledge desires that have been suppressed within themselves. It is also the case that the course of discovery experienced by Oedipus finds a correspondence in the process of self-discovery undertaken by the analysand in psychoanalysis.

Freud first used the term Oedipus complex in 1910, long after his account in *Interpreting Dreams* (1899) of why Sophocles' *Oedipus* makes such an impression on its audiences, and it has become such a familiar notion as to be conjured up merely by the word Oedipal. Apart from its use in a psychoanalytic context, where it has undergone a number of revisions and re-readings, references to the Oedipus complex nowadays are more likely to be tongue-in-cheek than as part of a serious attempt to understand someone's behaviour or motivation. What has not diminished, however, is the credence given to the force of the unconscious and, in a book entitled *Freud and Oedipus*, Peter Rudnytsky sees in Sophocles' play a conflicted Oedipus who has repressed the knowledge he cannot bring himself to openly admit. Where Vellacott saw Oedipus as secretly guarding what he knew to be the truth, Rudnytsky views him as burying the secret in his unconscious. Oedipus becomes angry with Teiresias because the seer draws attention to what he has repressed and, from this point of view, Oedipus and Teiresias represent 'two halves of a single psyche'.[27] Similarly, the Delphic oracle embodies the psychic compulsion that is driving Oedipus to combat his denial. Another psychoanalytic interpretation acknowledges Oedipus' Oedipal nature but also detects 'a narcissistic rage over his original mutilation and abandonment by his parents'.[28]

Oedipus in Ireland

W. B. Yeats, having helped to establish the Abbey Theatre in 1904, wanted to produce *Oedipus* at a time when the play was banned from the public stage in England but not in Ireland.[29] It had been performed in the original Greek at Cambridge in 1887, but its exposure in this way, to an elite university audience that was itself part of the Establishment, did as little to bother the authorities as it had six years earlier when the play in its original language had been performed by students of Harvard University in Cambridge,

Massachusetts. This had proved a tremendous success, witnessed by 6,000 people, and a detailed account of its production was published in 1882.[30]

Censorship of the public theatre (and at a time when incest had yet to be criminalized in England) could arouse ire – and the kind of withering remark made by the dramatist Henry Arthur Jones (1851–1929):

> Now of course, if any considerable body of Englishmen are arranging to marry their mothers, whether by accident or design, it must be stopped at once. But it is not a frequent occurrence in any class of English society. Throughout the course of my life I have not met more than six men who were anxious to do it.[31]

– and Yeats wanted *Oedipus* on an Irish stage, partly to expose a philistinism in the British Establishment ruling his country. Yeats approached Gilbert Murray and other possible translators but nothing came of it and the production that did appear on the Abbey stage in 1907, when Yeats had hoped *Oedipus* or another work by Sophocles would appear, was the famous riot-provoking performance of Synge's *The Playboy of the Western World*, a play also about parricide and written at a time when Synge was reading *Oedipus* and thinking about a production of it. Yeats decided he would work on his own version of the play, relying chiefly on Jebb's translation and one by Gilbert Murray which appeared in 1911. By this time the ban on performing the play in England had been lifted and Yeats saw Max Reinhardt's production of *Oedipus* in London in 1912, but his interest waned and fourteen years passed before he returned to the project and his version finally appeared on the Abbey stage in 1926. Yeats, who did not work from the original Greek, revised his text before it was published in 1928 and the final result is one of the more poetic adaptations of *Oedipus*.[32]

Yeats sought to contract and condense the play's fatalism down to its steely essence and make it, as he put it in a letter at the time, 'bare, hard and natural like a saga'.[33] He wanted a drama that was elemental, austere and elevated, repeating words where he felt the poetic effect could be heightened and, as with words given to the choral leader at the start of the play – 'For death is all the fashion now, till even Death be dead' – adding lines not to be found in the Greek.[34] When the play was performed in 1926 Yeats placed the chorus in the orchestral pit, with only the choral leader appearing on stage, an indication that his preferences lay more with the existential drama of an archetypal Everyman than an ancient Greek who commits incest in the *polis* of Thebes. The second antistrophe (179–202), depicting the communal grief of the city, is omitted entirely in favour of an invocation against death and cuts are made to the second stasimon (463–512) while allowing for an extended Yeatsian rendition of Jebb's faithful lines about 'snowy Parnassus' (475) and 'Earth's central shrine' (480):

> That sacred crossing-place of lines upon Parnassus' head,
> Lines that have run through North and South, and
> run through West and East,
> That navel of the world bids all men search the mountain wood.[35]

This has more to do with New Age mysticism and Yeats' gyres than with the original Greek but while he also chose to exclude most of Sophocles' lines that refer to incest (420–425, 457–46, 821–822 and 976) Yeats gives it an unexpectedly physical description when he comes to the chorus asking 'how have the furrows ploughed by your father endured to bear you' (1212):

> But looking for a marriage-bed, he found the bed of his birth,
> Tilled the field his father had tilled, cast seed into the same abounding earth;
> Entered through the door that had sent him wailing forth.[36]

The Sophoclean narrative is not altered, but the highly individual poetic inflection brought to Jebb's translation by Yeats makes his play an adaptation of the Greek drama. Despite this, it was treated more as a translation and remains very influential because of the way it has been used for a number of stage productions of *Oedipus*, including one at London's Old Vic in 1946 with a legendary performance by Laurence Olivier playing Oedipus,[37] one directed by Tyrone Guthrie in Canada in the 1950s and a production at Dublin's Abbey Theatre in 1972.[38] Tyrone Guthrie's production for the stage in Stratford, Ontario was subsequently filmed and released as *Oedipus Rex* in 1957. Guthrie's view of Sophocles' drama bears testimony to the way anthropological readings of Athenian drama continued to exert an influence in the 1950s: the film version begins with a narrator talking about the sacrifice of a king and in his *A Life in the Theatre* (1960) Guthrie referred to 'the sacred drama of *Oedipus Rex* . . . [in which the actor] impersonates a symbol of sacrifice'.[39] In directing *Oedipus* he did not seek realistic effect and with the actors wearing large masks, psychologically convincing performances were not being strived for.

Two other Irish writers, Derek Mahon and Frank McGuinness, have worked on Sophocles' *Oedipus*. Derek Mahon conflates Sophocles' *Oedipus* and *Oedipus at Colonus* into one, seeing them 'as a single play united by the arc of Oedipus' fate',[40] and makes changes to the text to fit this unitary approach. So, for example, when Oedipus is disconcerted by the blind prophet's mention of his parents (435ff.), Fagles gives a fairly literal translation of Teiresias' reply to Oedipus' demand for more information: 'This day will bring your birth and your destruction.' Mahon, writing a play that encompasses events at Colonus taking place many years later, renders the reply within a longer time span: 'You are born today; a strange new life begins.'[41]

Frank McGuiness produced his version for the National Theatre, directed by Jonathan Kent, staged in modern dress with Ralph Fiennes playing Oedipus. It opened on the stage in 2008 and while it was well received by some theatre critics, this was not everyone's opinion and for some it was a flat and unmoving experience, due not to the quality of the acting but to the nature of the production and an uneven, conventional text.[42] In 1996, Peter Hall had produced an impressive version of *Oedipus* at the same theatre, using masked actors and highly ritualized movements, but the 2008 production was very different and very un-Greek, with a chorus of fourteen men in modern grey suits. McGuiness has spoken of Sophocles' play as 'deeply masculine, terribly male' and his version for the National Theatre version as a personal 'cry of pain' for his own father's death.[43]

Oedipus in the vernacular

In Stephen Berkoff's, *Greek*, first performed in 1980, the tragic hero of ancient Thebes becomes a non-tragic hero in 1980s London; there is no space here for Freud but with one very important exception: most of the essential elements of Sophocles' play find a modern correspondence. There is a gypsy fortune teller who foretells a violent death for a child's father and 'something worse than death / and that's a bunk-up with his mum', and the plague becomes the deprivation and poverty of Eddy's environment. Eddy leaves home and one day in an altercation with the manager of a café kills him and later marries his wife, telling her, 'I think we're fated love don't you?' Fate is also evoked by his parents who had wondered if they should have told Eddy how he was adopted by them: 'it can't be now undone with words / fate makes us play the roles we're cast.' Eddy solves the riddle of the Sphinx, its last part given a priapic twist ('in the evenings when he is erect for his woman he sprouts the third leg'), and becomes a successful, happily married man. There is a recognition scene when Eddy's parents tell him how he was adopted and his wife realizes how this accords with how she lost a son years earlier. Eddy is aghast – 'Me who wants to clean up the city / stop the plague destroy the Sphinx / me was the source of all the stink / the man of principle is a motherfucker' – but decides to stay with his wife/mother: 'We only love so it doesn't matter mother, mother it doesn't matter. Why should I tear my eyes out Greek style, why should you hang yourself?' As Berkoff explains:

> Oedipus found a city in the grip of a plague and sought to rid the city of its evil centre represented by the Sphinx. Eddy seeks to reaffirm his beliefs and inculcate a new order of things with his vision and life-affirming energy. His passion for life is inspired by the love he feels for his woman, and his detestation of the degrading environment he inherited. If Eddy is a warrior who holds up the smoking sword as he goes in, attacking all that he finds polluted, at the same time he is at heart an ordinary young man with whom many I know will find identification.[44]

Berkoff has also written *Oedipus*, his own version of Sophocles' play, and directed its production at the Liverpool Playhouse in 2011. Though this time Berkoff uses iambic pentameters, the use of the vernacular is the play's distinctive feature and so we hear Creon reply to Oedipus' wish to have the news he brings back from Delphi announced in public:

OK – no sweat – I'll give it to you straight . . .
He says, cut out the monstrous growth within.[45]

When such a style is pursued relentlessly, it becomes difficult to differentiate the dramatic voices at work in the play and Berkoff's chorus, responding to the altercation between Teiresias and Oedipus, does not sound very different to other characters:

Anyone can shout and spew
But I'm uneasy
I'll not convict
Oedipus! Guilty?
It doesn't fit.[46]

Such a no-nonsense way of speaking also epitomizes Oedipus' approach to life, in keeping with the way Berkoff understands him:

I see Oedipus as a modern man, self-made, tough and bold, who uses language as a weapon to cut through verbal adiposity and obliqueness. He is more of a strutter whose stance relates to him having always to battle against some force determined to defeat him.[47]

In Berkoff's play Oedipus attains a kind of tragic status when he resolutely opposes the force of fate and insists on controlling his own life when the truth is revealed. The gods are to blame for what has happened and by blinding himself he asserts his independence:

Now I will be the master of my fate,
I will no longer witness what you've done,
I take your world away.[48]

Another version of *Oedipus*, written by Blake Morrison for the Northern Broadsides Theatre Company and premiered in Halifax in 2001, shifts the locale to northern England. Morrison explains how he wanted to 'cut away the dead wood' of academically minded translations and find 'spurts of life, the saplings that we could grow something from'.[49] Such radical stem-cell surgery sounds too alarming for its own good, more like the creation of a Frankenstein than a modern revival of an ancient classic, but a review of the stage production by Edith Hall found reason to praise Morrison's 'muscular, caustic and knowing poetic dialect' and felt it did some justice to the original because he realizes 'that the tragic power of the original is predicated on the audience's experience of pleasurable language'.[50] To take an example, the words of Oedipus to the distraught Jocasta who has realized the truth and is desperately trying to prevent him from also knowing it are translated by Jebb: 'Be of good courage; though I be found the son of servile mother, – aye, a slave by three descents, – *thou* wilt not be proved base-born' (1060–1062). This is close to the original Greek and while Jebb lends it a certain archaism it is not difficult, as Ruth Fainlight does in her translation, to turn it into modern English:

> Be brave woman! Even if I am proved three times a slave, from three generations of slaves, that will not make you base-born.

When it comes to these lines Morrison does not depart from the meaning of the Greek, but gives them a clear colloquial inflection:

> Why should you suffer? Your ancestry's secure.
> The lines in your brow run back centuries.
> If it turns out my mum, nan and great-gran
> Were all slaves, it won't be any skin off your nose,
> It won't make the blood in your veins any less blue.

This can be taken to be in accord with Morrison's dictum that 'The classics always adapt; that's why they're classics. But the adaptor who doesn't respect the spirit of the original is irresponsible and self-defeating,'[51] and one can stretch this statement of intent to include lines like 'You're as dainty as an otter with a salmon in its maw' (Oedipus speaking to Creon). Perhaps though, what makes Morrison's play an adaptation rather than a translation is not the making of Oedipus into a bluff and bolshie Yorkshireman but the psychologizing that is brought into the text as an accompaniment to this characterization. In the account Oedipus gives of his encounter with Laius at the crossroads, it is not the added details or the language that detract from 'the spirit of the original' but the interiorization, the 'voice' of motivation and class-consciousness that is absent from Sophocles' Oedipus at this moment in the drama.

> . . . there I am,
> sun beaming down, scrats of cloud in the sky,
> minding my own, pondering which road to take,
> when along comes a coach party – a driver,
> two men on horseback, a messenger boy
> running ahead, and a man inside the carriage,
> just as you said. There's plenty of room to pass,
> but the driver and the bigwig inside
> scream at me to clear out the bloody way.
> If only they'd ask nicely I'd not mind,
> but when the driver tries to force me off the road
> I see red and fetch him full in the face,
> and then the old fellow inside the carriage
> leans out and raddles me with a spiked club
> or something and keeps thumping me over the head
> till I lose patience and learn him a lesson,
> my blows are flisky little tigs, that's all,
> but before I know it he's reeling under 'em,
> he's rolling through the door of the carriage,
> he's laid out on his back eyeing the heavens
> and the body I'm battering is a corpse.

The narrative of *The Gods Are Not to Blame*, written by the Nigerian dramatist Ola Rotimi and first published in 1971, is told in a very different vernacular while remaining remarkably faithful to Sophocles' play. It tells the tale of Odewale, the son of King Adetusa and Queen Ojuola, whose life story parallels that of Oedipus in many important respects. Odewale helps the people of Kutuje defeat their tribal enemy and, following their custom, marries Queen Ojuola without realizing she is his mother. Years later, a mysterious sickness afflicts his new community and Odewale vows to find the killer of their late king. Long before these events, having run away from what was his foster home, after being told he was not the son of his supposed father, Odewale had settled elsewhere as a farmer, but found himself in a tribal quarrel over land and killed a man who turns out to be his father. Soothsayers inform Odewale of his fate and provide his parents with a prophecy that causes them to react in the same kind of way as Laius and Jocasta did when they received similar news. The truth is gradually revealed and the play ends with Odewale blinding himself, after Ojuola commits suicide, and he leaves the village with his children, laying a curse on anyone who tries to stop him.

The Gods Are Not to Blame is conventionally read as a metaphorical tale of intertribal warfare and in particular as a comment on the Nigerian civil war of 1966.[52] While not discounting this dimension to the play – in his final words Odewale sees tribal loyalty as the cause of the tragedy – Rotimi's drama has also been situated within a post-colonial context and given an additional political edge.[53]

Rita Dove's *The Darker Face of the Earth* offers another response to Sophocles' *Oedipus* by an African-American playwright. First performed in 1996, the play is set in pre-Civil War South Carolina where Amalia, wife to a plantation owner, gave birth to a slave's child but had little choice but to allow his adoption. Augustus, the name of her son, turns up as a slave many years later and, their kinship unknown to both of them, is seduced by Amalia. When the truth emerges, Augustus kills his father and Amalia commits suicide. There is a sorcerer slave, Scylla, who identifies the birth of Augustus with something accursed and her conflict with him mirrors the vexed relationship between Teiresias and Oedipus in Sophocles. Paralleling the defeat of the Sphinx's riddle by the rational Oedipus, Augustus confronts the fears and superstitions of his fellow slaves, mocks their Christian worship – 'Listen to them sing! What kind of god preaches such misery?' – and the cryptic warnings of Scylla:

> Women like her, hah!
> They get a chill one morning,
> Hear an owl or two, and snap!
> They've received their 'powers'!
> Then they collect a few old bones,
> Dry some herbs, and they're in business.[54]

Augustus plans a slave revolt while the presence of Scylla, whose incantations are laced with Yoruba expressions, stands as an emblem of African spiritual values and a maternal compassion that opposes male violence: 'What will these people do with your hate after you free them – as you promise?'[55] Scylla's insight does not detract from the central truth of the play: the institution of slavery is the equivalence of the plague that afflicted Thebes and its corrosive consequences are the cause of tragedy.[56]

Literary fiction

Echoes of *Oedipus* have been heard in an eclectic range of literary fiction, including Flannery O'Connor's *Wise Blood*, a novel about a disturbed and very strange preacher in America's rural South who seeks proselytes for his Church Without Christ but with little success.[57] Hazel Motes, the preacher, eventually blinds himself but whether, like Oedipus, he learns something important about his own identity is questionable. Flannery O'Connor completed her novel when she was living in the home of Robert Stewart Fitzgerald, a poet who at the time was working on a translation of Sophocles' play, and so she may well have been influenced by the Greek classic. Similarities with *Oedipus* are more straightforwardly discerned in literary fiction like Max Frisch's *Homo Faber* where the leading character, Walter, comes to discover that the woman he has formed a relationship with, and had sex with, is his daughter. Walter is a technologist by profession, and his view of himself and the world gradually frays as circumstances compel him to question his identity and outlook on life. In the course of events unfolded in the novel he comes to redefine himself as a result of meeting again the woman who was the mother of his daughter.

In Kleist's comic play, *The Broken Jug*, the judge responsible for establishing the guilt or innocence of the man accused of breaking a jug, highly valued by its owner and whose daughter's virtue is also on trial, is himself to blame for the offence(s) being investigated. The judge, like the audience, knows this full well and his attempts at concealment gradually lead to the uncovering of the truth. There is an explicit reference to Sophocles by Kleist in a note to his play and echoes of *Oedipus* can be traced in *The Broken Jug*, not least in the significance attached to feet. Kleist's comedy has been adapted by John Banville, transposing the events from a German village to an Irish one and providing a colonial context for the humour which allows Banville to indulge in some mild racism at his own country's expense. Blake Morrison has also adapted the play, this time to early nineteenth-century Skipton, and as with his version of *Oedipus* he renders its humour in earthy Yorkshire dialect.

A novel where a parallel with *Oedipus* is explicit rather than just implied is Alain Robbe-Grillet's *The Erasers* (*Les Gommes*), published like *Wise Blood* and *Homo Faber* in the 1950s. In the story, Daniel Dupont is shot but not killed by an intruder and arranges with a doctor to have himself declared dead. Wallas, the policeman investigating the supposed murder of Dupont, spends a day looking for clues and goes to Dupont's house in the evening. Dupont himself returns to his house at the same time to retrieve some papers and Wallas, drawing his gun, shoots him dead at 7.30pm. This was the time, twenty four hours earlier, when his watch had stopped working but it now starts running again and telling the correct time. Wallas had been missing vital information about the case he was working on – the fact that Dupont is not dead – and he only learns the truth at the point where he becomes the killer he seeks. This kind of surprise ending is familiar in detective stories – it can be found in Agatha Christie's *The Murder of Roger Ackroyd* when Hercule Poirot reveals the murderer to be his assistant, Dr. Sheppard, and the story's narrator – and does not by itself make Robbe-Grillet's novel a version of *Sophocles'* drama. The novel, however, takes its epigram from *Oedipus* and there is no shortage in the text of explicit pointers to Sophocles' tale: Wallas suffers from swollen feet after a long day spent walking the streets, there is a drunk who speak in riddles, a Corinth Street, a window display depicting ancient Greece, and other references that make it clear the novelist is consciously playing with *Oedipus*.[58] *The Erasers*, in a way, inverts Sophocles' *Oedipus* (where Oedipus discovers the truth behind the fiction that Laius was murdered by a robber or robbers) by making true a fiction (the supposed death of Dupont).

Fiction like *The Erasers* brings to the reader's mind the story of Oedipus as told in ancient myth but does not evoke the world of ancient Greece or suggest empathy with the concerns of Sophocles' play. Salley Vickers *Where Three Roads Meet* is different in this respect and her novel does engage with *Oedipus* in a convincing and thoughtful manner. The story is set in London, September 1938, where the dying Freud, in exile from Nazi-occupied Europe, is periodically visited by Teiresias. In the course of their conversations Teiresias relates the uncanny events that inspired the psychoanalyst's famous theory while Freud, a twentieth-century unbeliever in divination, interjects with clinical and clipped observations of a suitably Freudian nature. The psychoanalyst has one explanation for Oedipus' self-blinding; the seer another:

> – It was castration, of course. The eyes and the male member; it is well established from the study of dreams that the two are synonyms.
> – No, Dr Freud. Had Oedipus seen fit to castrate himself, believe me he would have done so. It was shame. Like a child who hides his hands he supposed that if he couldn't see the world, the world could not see him. It wasn't that he didn't want to see – it was, in the horror of recognition, the horror of being recognized.[59]

Opera and ballet

Opera as an art form combining text and music was invented with Greek drama in mind and the Florentines who inspired the form were not only conscious of the fact that the chorus in Athenian tragedies sang its lines, but were given to thinking that perhaps all of the dramatic text was delivered in this way. The earliest known work considered as an opera, *Dafne*, was written in 1597 around the story of Apollo falling in love with the nymph Daphne and the earliest surviving opera, *Eurydice*, composed three years later, is also based on a Greek myth.

The best known operatic version of *Oedipus* is by Stravinsky, first performed in Paris in 1927 as an oratorio although it was also composed for production on the stage as an opera. It was first filmed when Leonard Bernstein conducted it in London in 1973 and filmed again in 1992 for a production in Japan. The libretto was written by Jean Cocteau at Stravinsky's request, but the composer was not happy with the result and he pared it down himself before having it translated into Latin: 'The choice [of Latin] had the great advantage of giving me a medium not dead but turned to stone and so monumentalised as to have become immune from all risk of vulgarisation.'[60] The context of impersonality that Stravinsky was seeking for his music, and for an authentic evocation of Athenian drama,[61] emerges from the way he envisaged the chorus in his opera-oratorio as seated and monk-like in its stillness, wearing cowls and reading from scrolls, while most of the characters, including Oedipus, move only their arms and heads. This was part of the Apollonian order that Stravinsky, consciously using Nietzsche's terms, saw as merging with the Dionysian register of the music:

> What is important for the lucid ordering of the work . . . is that all the Dionysian elements which set the imagination of the artist in motion and make the life-sap rise must be properly subjugated before they intoxicate us, and must finally be made to submit to the law: Apollo demands it.[62]

Cocteau went on to write his own version of the Oedipus myth, *The Infernal Machine*, a highly theatrical and Freud-inspired play which starts with a *Hamlet*-like scene featuring the ghost of Laius appearing on the ramparts of Thebes, and it makes plain the aesthetic gulf between Stravinsky and Cocteau:

> Stravinsky instinctively sensed the monumental qualities of the play [Sophocles'], its subordination of character to fate, and where Cocteau, in his interspersed narration ('Il tombe. Il tombe de haut'), tries to milk the pathos of Oedipus' tragic discovery that he is the polluter, Stravinsky's music wonderfully keeps alive Sophocles' sense that if this is a disaster for Oedipus it is nonetheless the salvation of the city of Thebes.[63]

Not as well known as Stravinsky's work, and rarely performed, George Enescu's opera *Oedipe* is based on *Oedipus* and has been ranked 'the only significant and illuminating response to Sophocles' *Oedipus the King*'.[64] It was begun in 1910, after the composer had seen a production of *Oedipus*, and completed twelve years later, although it was not performed until 1936. Some 350 players were involved in this performance, with its third act covering the story of Sophocles' *Oedipus*. Another opera, *Oedipus*, by the composer

Harry Partch (1901–1974) found inspiration in Yeats' text but when Partch lost the rights to perform it using Yeats' words for the libretto he wrote a new text and used this for performances. The most recent opera inspired by *Oedipus*, although circuitously, is Mark-Anthony Turnage's *Greek* based on the Steven Berkoff play and with a libretto adapted by Turnage and Jonathan Moore from Berkoff's *Greek*. Turnage was commissioned to write a piece for the first Munich Biennale in 1988, where it received its premiere and won the prizes for best opera and best libretto. It was later filmed by the BBC. Given the nature of Berkoff's *Greek*, the opera was inevitably considered outré and it established Turnage's reputation. The self-blinding of Oedipus does not occur in Berkoff's play but the opera alludes to it more directly with a mime scene where Eddy, the Oedipus-figure who has discovered the truth about his identity, does blind himself and dies. In keeping with the spirit of Berkoff's *Greek*, though, the funeral procession that gets underway is undercut by Eddy's 'Bollocks to all that' and his resolve to go on loving his wife and mother.[65]

Martha Graham's *Night Journey*, premièred in 1947, reconfigures *Oedipus* play into a dance drama that explores and expresses the mostly missing erotic dimension to Sophocles' tale. Graham's method of achieving this is by making Jocasta the central character and the dance begins with her in the centre of the stage holding the rope that she will later use to kill herself. Before this, however, she journeys back into a world of desire and dreams where Oedipus makes a triumphant appearance, joyfully greeted by a female chorus, and the two of them make love in a sequence of movements that aspires to conjoin the husband/wife and mother/son relationship. André Boucourechliev's *Le Nom d'Oedipe*, an opera, probably even less well known than Enescu's *Oedipe*, is not altogether different in this respect though this time it is not the erotic element that comes to the fore. First performed in 1978, with Hélène Cixous writing the libretto, *Le Nom d'Oedipe*, shares with Graham's *Night Journey* an interest in feminist, psychoanalytic currents that never rise to the surface in Sophocles but which can be read back into the story of Oedipus. Jocasta is again the protagonist as she relives –

'the loss of the forbidden body that she enjoyed in the pre-Oedipal state she shared with her son . . . not incest that is taboo here; instead it is the Cartesian mind/body divide that is derided by Boucourechliev and Cixous.[66]

Film & TV

The first film of the Oedipus story was made in France in 1912, entitled *The Legend of Oedipus*, but this silent film has been lost and the only visual evidence that remains of it are a few production stills. It is known that when the film was shown in Germany, six scenes – those involving the killing of Laius and the Sphinx, Jocasta's suicide and Oedipus' blinding – had to be cut from it in order to satisfy the censor.[67]

The film version of Tyrone Guthrie's production of *Oedipus*, released as *Oedipus Rex* in 1957, has already been mentioned. A third film version, directed by Philip Saville in 1967, used the ancient amphitheatre at Dodoni in Greece for its location and its star included Orson Welles as Teiresias and Donald Sutherland (though his voice was dubbed) as the choral leader.

The most memorable film of *Oedipus* is Pasolini's *Edipo Re*, released in 1967. The setting is a strange mix of twentieth-century Italy, moving from the 1930s to the 1960s, and an ancient, primitive world of myth evoked by filming in a North African desert and using outlandish costumes and very unhomely music. The main narrative remains fairly faithful to Sophocles' story but there is a radical transformation from the portrayal of Oedipus as a thoughtful, rational man determined to solve a puzzle into a creature governed by impulse and chance. When Oedipus decides not to return to Corinth after visiting Delphi, his choice of where to go is settled by blindly whirling himself around and heading off in whatever direction he faces when he opens his eyes. The encounter with Laius is also enacted as if the two antagonists are in the grip of forces they cannot acknowledge and are simply obliged to engage violently with one another. The sphinx asks a personal question – 'There is an enigma in your life, what is it?' – which Oedipus violently rejects: 'I don't want to know it'.

The film creates the strong sense of an archaic primitivism governing people's behaviour, flavoured with an occasional heavy dose of Freudianism as in the early scenes with Oedipus as a baby. The film shows him being born and breastfed by his thoughtful and slightly perturbed mother and then, as an infant, exchanging looks with his father and the words 'you are here to take my place, send me again into the void, and rob me of all I have' appearing on the screen. With the camera focused on the troubled-looking father, further words appear – 'she will be the first thing you rob from me, see the woman I love, already you steal her love' – and, after making love with his wife, the father lifts the infant up from his bed by his ankles. The next scene shows the infant Oedipus being carried into the desert and abandoned there only to be found by a passing shepherd.

While Pasolini is directly and obviously working from *Oedipus* in his film, Park Chan-wook only mentions Sophocles as one of the influences on his work. But his film, *Oldboy*, brings *Oedipus* to mind in ways that are more resonant than *Edipo Re*. In the film, Oh Dae-su is snatched off a street and kept in a private prison for fifteen years, never being told who has put him there or why. Determined to break out, his escape plan becomes redundant when he is suddenly released and left to pursue a vengeful search for his unknown enemy. He encounters a young girl, Mi-do, and they fall in love. There is nothing to suggest a connection with *Oedipus* until Dae-su finds himself able to kill his oppressor, Woo-jin, but only at the cost of not finding out why he was imprisoned. His desire to establish the truth is too strong and, even though it imperils Mi-do's life, chooses to pursue further his investigations. Such persistence, as with *Oedipus*, causes his downfall because it leads to a discovery of past events and identities, including his own, that he was tragically unaware of. His act of incest is revealed when, in a moment of *peripeteia* (reversal) that Aristotle would have recognized, he learns that Mi-do is his daughter at the same time as discovering that a youthful error of judgement on his part led to his long incarceration. Oedipus' reaction is to cut out his eyes – 'they will never see the crime I have committed or had done upon me!' (1271–1272) – and Dae-su cuts out his tongue so that he will not be able to speak again (it was his loose talk that had caused the suicide of Woo-jin's sister). And just as Oedipus comes to view his tragedy as occasioned by both Apollo and his own past action committed in ignorance (1329–1333), Dae-su realizes that his catastrophe is attributable to both an external force beyond his control (Woo-jin employed hypnosis to help Mi-do and Dae-su fall in love) and his own behaviour committed in ignorance as a youth.

Chan-wook's film is not setting out to be a version of Sophocles' drama and there are important elements to *Oldboy* that do not relate to *Oedipus*; nonetheless the two works share a concern with issues of self-knowledge, unintentionality and chance and they both express and explore these concerns in ways that render them tragedies. *Oldboy* ends with Dae-su asking the hypnotist to help him forget what has happened and she agrees, but the film's final shot, showing Dae-su's intensely anguished face as he embraces Mi-do, leaves open just how successful the hypnosis has been. The audience is left with the feelings of pity and fear that Aristotle identified as the emotional and cognitive basis of a tragedy.

There are two notable productions of *Oedipus* that were made for television: a BBC *King Oedipus* in 1972, directed by Alan Bridges, and a 1984 *Oedipus the King* directed by Don Taylor (who also translated the play), starring Michael Pennington as Oedipus. A mention should also be made of two films by Claude Berri, *Jean De Florette* and *Manon Des Sources*, based on the novels by Marcel Pagnol, that have been seen to echo aspects of the Oedipus tale.[68]

Notes

1   Herder (1985), pp. 161–176.

2   The first printed edition was in 1474, but its influence has been traced back to a production over a century earlier. See Seneca (1966), pp. 26ff.

3   Seneca (1966), 78 (p. 212); 76–77 (p. 211).

4   Ibid., 1056–1061 (p. 251).

5   Eliot (1956), pp. 6–7.

6   Harrison (2000).

7   Hughes (1969), p. 8.

8   Ibid.

9   Hughes (1972), p, 77.

10   Corneille (1980–1987), V, 9, (2004–2005).

11   Voltaire (1877).

12   Burian (1997), p. 247.

13   Hölderlin (2001), p. 28.

14   Fóti (2006), p. 107.

15   Ibid., p. 67.

16   Ibid., 49.

17   Ibid, p. 67.

18   Quoted from Fynsk (1993), p. 257; see also, http://glennwallis.com/blog/tag/friedrich-holderlin (accessed 1 October 2011).

19   Nietzsche (2000), p. 54 (Section 9).

20   Ibid., p. 55.

21   Ibid., p. 53.

22   Heidegger (2000), p. 112.

23   Ibid., pp. 112–113.

24   In his memoirs, Mounet-Sully gave his own view of the role he was playing: 'In Oedipus I had seen a man who revolts against his destiny, who is proud of his power. He disputes the orders of the gods; he does not submit himself to the prophecies. In wanting to avoid them, he makes them come true, and he falls in the trap laid for him by the gods who are jealous of their authority. This strong man contains the quintessence of a humanity that is proud and rebellious against the Divine. He is a sort of Prometheus who will never see the vulture, and each of his cries is like the shaking of invisible chains. Oedipus represents the revolt of instinct and intelligence against blind fate and man's final defeat.' Quoted from Armstrong (1999).

25   Jones (1953), p. 177.

26   Freud (2006), p. 276. In his *Introductory Lectures on psychoanalysis* Freud emphasizes the 'secret' nature of the play's appeal: 'It is surprising that Sophocles' tragedy does not call forth indignant remonstrance in its audience . . . For at bottom it's an immoral play; it sets aside the individual's responsibility to social law and displays divine forces ordaining the crime and rendering powerless the moral instincts of the human being which would guard him against the crime. It would be easy to believe that an accusation against destiny and the gods was intended in the story of the myth . . . But with the reverent Sophocles there is no question of such an intention; the pious subtlety which declares it the highest morality to bow to the will of the gods, even when they ordain a crime, helps him out of the difficulty. I do not believe that this moral is one of the virtues of the drama, but neither does it detract from its effect; it leaves the hearer indifferent; he does not react to this, but to the secret meaning and content of the myth itself. He reacts as though by self-analysis he had detected the Oedipus complex in himself, and had recognized the will of the gods

and the oracle as glorified disguises of his own unconscious.' Quoted from Dawe (2006), p. 2.

27   Rudnytsky (1987), p. 269.

28   Lee Miller (2007), p. 229.

29   This was before Gilbert Murray advised Yeats not to go near Euripides because he was not sufficiently Irish and to look instead to Sophocles (suggesting *The Persians* and *Prometheus Bound*).

30   'After a short pause the great doors of the palace are thrown back, and the attendants of Oedipus enter and take up their positions on each side. They wear thin lavender tunics reaching nearly to the knee. Their looks are directed at the interior of the palace, whence, in a moment, Oedipus enters. His royal robes gleam now with the purple of silk and now with the red of gold; gold embroidery glitters on his crimson tunic and on his white sandals; his gown gives him dignity and height.' Norman (2010), pp. 68–69.

31   Quoted in Clark and McGuire (1989), p. 3.

32   For comparisons of Yeats's play with Jebb's translation that he worked from, see Grab (1972) and Macintosh (2008).

33   Foster (2003), p. 338.

34   Yeats (1967), p. 480.

35   Ibid., p. 488.

36   Ibid., p. 511.

37   'As the blinded King Oedipus he uttered a terrible, desolate scream of pain which I shall always remember, and I remember his telling me how he came by it. "First of all", he said, "I thought of foxes. Little foxes with their paws caught in a trap." He held out his wrists helplessly. "And then I heard about how they catch ermine. It was a great help to me when I heard about that. In the Arctic they put down salt and the ermine comes to lick it. It's caught when its tongue freezes to the ice. I thought about that sudden pain when I screamed as Oedipus."' John Mortimer remembering Laurence Olivier speak of his performance as Oedipus (http://www.nationaltheatre.org. uk/11553/laurence-olivier/john-mortimer-remembers-sir-laurence-olivier.html, accessed 1 October 2011).

38   Yeats' version was also going to be used for the stage production, with Al Pacino playing Oedipus at the Actors Studio in New York, that was being planned in 2000 but which never came to fruition.

39   Quoted from Macintosh (2008), p. 541.

40   Mahon (2005), p. 9.

41 Ibid., p. 25.

42 There was also the irony of a play about Theban land suffering ecological ruin (the consequence of one kind of pollution) being sponsored by an international oil company, Shell, associated with ecological ruin brought about by a different kind of pollution. www.indymedia.org.uk/en/2008/10/411200.html (accessed 1 October 2011).

43 Quoted from an interview available at http://podcasts.ox.ac.uk (accessed 1 October 2011).

44 Berkoff (1994), p. 97.

45 Berkoff (2000), p. 162.

46 Ibid., p. 180.

47 Ibid., p. 155.

48 Ibid., p. 209.

49 Quoted from Northern Broadsides' education pack for their production at www.northern-broadsides.co.uk (accessed 1 October 2011).

50 Ibid.

51 Morrison (2010), p. 256.

52 Wetmore (2002).

53 Simpson (2010); Goff and Simpson (2007), pp. 78–134.

54 Dove (1999), p. 40.

55 Ibid., p. 93.

56 Carlisle (2000); Goff and Simpson (2007), pp. 135–177.

57 Moddelmog (1993), pp. 90–94.

58 Morrissette (1960).

59 Vickers (2008), p. 176.

60 Quoted from White (1966), p. 290.

61 'The way to recreate classic dramas is to cool them, to bring them closer by making them more distant,' quoted from Arnott (1959), p. 231.

62 Stravinsky (1974), pp. 80–81.

63 Josipovici (2010), p. 160. The action confined to Sophocles' play, the detective work by Oedipus and his self-blinding, occupy only the final part of Cocteau's play and the rest of his drama is devoted to the appearance of the ghost of Laius, the defeat of the Sphinx and the wedding night of Oedipus and Jocasta.

64   Ewans (2007), p. 106.

65   A new production of Turnage's *Greek*, by Music Theatre Wales, toured Britain between July and November 2011. Stephen Berkoff directed a production of his own play *Greek* for the Liverpool Playhouse and the Edinburgh Festival Fringe in 2011.

66   Macintosh (2009), p. 185.

67   Hall and Harrop (2010), pp. 99–101.

68   Rabel (2009).

CHAPTER SEVEN

Guide to further reading

Editions of *Oedipus*

A translation of *Oedipus* by David Grene in *Sophocles 1*, edited by Grene and Lattimore, identifies the strophes and antistrophes in the chorus' lines. This is the edition used in this book, unless stated otherwise, for quotations in English from *Oedipus*.

Another translation, by Stephen Berg and Diskin Clay, that is also part of a two-volume set, *The Complete Sophocles*, edited by Peter Burian and Alan Shapiro, indicates the division between strophes and antistrophes only by line breaks but, unlike Grene's translation, makes clear that Oedipus' lines beginning at 1208 are sung in response to the chorus.

The translation by H. D. F. Kitto in the Oxford World Classics *Sophocles: Antigone, Oedipus the King and Electra*, edited by Edith Hall, identifies by headings whether choral lines are a strophe or antistrophe and also clearly indicates when lines are sung or spoken.

Among the other editions of *Oedipus* in translation, Robert Fagles' in *The Three Theban Plays* for Penguin Classics (1984) should not be confused with the 1947 translation by E. F. Watling which is also published by Penguin as *The Theban Plays*. More recent translations of note include one by Don Taylor in *Sophocles Plays: One*, in a series edited by J. Michael Walton for Methuen, but no line numbering is used. In a series of translations of Greek dramas, published by Cambridge University Press, one of *Oedipus* by Ian McAuslan and Judith Affleck (with line numbering) includes a useful commentary alongside each page of the text.

Other translations include ones by David Mulroy (University of Wisconsin Press), Ruth Fainlight and Robert Littman (The John Hopkins University Press), and one by Frederick Ahl (Cornell University Press) that is paired with a translation of Seneca's *Oedipus*. The extensive introduction by Ahl goes over, in a more succinct form, the thesis concerning Oedipus' innocence advanced in his 'Sophocles' Oedipus: Evidence & Self-Conviction'.

There are two dual Greek and English editions of *Oedipus*: one edited and translated by Hugh Lloyd-Jones came out in 1994 (reprinted with corrections in 1997) for the Loeb series of classical texts; the other one, by R. C. Jebb and first published in the late nineteenth century (see page 118), remains a very readable and useful edition for studying the play and is available online through The Perseus digital library (www.perseus.tufts.edu) as well as in print editions. An edition of *Oedipus* in Greek, part of The Oxford Classical Texts series, edited by Hugh Lloyd-Jones and N. G. Wilson, was published in 1990. An edition of the Greek text with a detailed commentary, edited by R. D. Dawe, was first published in 1982 by Cambridge University Press and its revised edition of 2006 has become the standard reference for readers.

The language and style of *Oedipus* in English can vary considerably according to, among other factors, the measure of imaginative licence assumed by the translator and the degree of poetic talent they bring to their task. As an example, take the lines spoken by the chorus in the second strophe of the parode (175–177) where they use an image of birds in flight for the death-in-life of stillborn children, victims of the plague:

> *allon d' an allō prosidois haper eupteron ornin*
> *kreisson amaimaketou puros ormenon*
> *aktan pros hesperou theou.*

Jebb's Victorian rendition gives us:

> and life on life mayest thou see sped, like bird
> on nimble wing, aye, swifter than resistless
> fire, to the shore of the western god.

His last line is a literal translation of the Greek for, as Edith Hall puts it in the notes to the Oxford World Classics edition, 'the home of the shades of the dead was traditionally located towards the setting sun' (e.g. Homer, *Odyssey* 12.81).[1] Berg and Clay feel that the suddenness of departing lives is best expressed in more abrupt lines –

> and lives one after another split the air
> birds taking off
> wingrush hungrier than fire
> souls leaping away they fly
> to the shore
> of the cold god of evening
> west

– while Fagles strives to draw a picture of Sophocles' image in words –

> and life on life goes down
> you can watch them go
> like seabirds winging west, outracing the day's fire
> down the horizon, irresistibly
> streaking on to the shores of Evening
> Death

– and the translation by Ahl seems closely modelled on Fagles:

> Look! For if you did, you'd see
> life after life surging
> like birds with powerful wings, more irresistibly
> than raging fire
> to the sunset god's edge of death

Background

A good place to begin is with three essays – 'The Origins of Theatre' by Winnington-Ingram, 'Theatre in Performance' by John Gould and 'Sophocles' by Easterling – in *The Cambridge History of Classical Literature*, edited by Easterling and Knox.

They provide a judicious assessment of what is known about how tragedy developed, its place in the Athenian community and what can be surmised about how they were performed based on archaeological evidence, ancient accounts and the plays themselves. Easterling's essay on Sophocles is a useful overview of the dramatist's work.

Rabinowitz's *Greek Tragedy* provides a helpful introduction and each of the sections in the first part of the book – 'What was Tragedy', 'Tragedy and the *Polis*', 'Tragedy and Greek Religion' – concludes with suggestions for further reading. The second part of the book has chapters on different Greek tragedies, including *Oedipus*.

Edmunds' *Oedipus*, part of a 'Gods and Heroes of the Ancient World' series, looks at the ways in which the myths associated with Oedipus were presented in the ancient world and the continuing influence of these myths in modern literature and other art forms. An essay by Richard Buxton, 'Tragedy and Greek Myth', in *The Cambridge Companion to Greek Mythology*, serves as a good introduction to its subject although it does not focus on Sophocles' *Oedipus*.

Two texts are recommended for an understanding of the form of Athenian tragedy: the book *On Aristotle and Greek Tragedy* by John Jones and an essay by John Gould in his *Myth, Ritual, Memory and Exchange*, 'Dramatic Character and "Human Intelligibility" in Greek Tragedy'.

Sophocles' *Oedipus*

Two books bring together various critical essays and selections from books about *Oedipus: Twentieth-Century Interpretations of Oedipus Rex*, edited by O'Brien, and *Bloom's Modern Critical Interpretations: Oedipus Rex*, edited by Harold Bloom. Both include E. R. Dodd's influential 'On Misunderstanding the Oedipus Rex' and an excerpt from Fergusson's *The Idea of a Theater*, but Bloom's collection, appearing more than twenty years after O'Brien's, includes more recent critical voices.

There are a number of books by Charles Segal offering in-depth studies of *Oedipus* and the best one of these, *Oedipus Tyrannus: Tragic Heroism and the Limits of Knowledge* (first published in

1993, revised and expanded in the second edition of 2001), gives a scene-by-scene analysis of the text.

Rush Rehm's *The Play of Space*, based 'on the simple premise that space is a proper value of the theater, part and parcel of what it is and how it works'[2], has a chapter ('Space, Time, and Memory') on *Oedipus*.

For a post-Freudian psychoanalytic reading of *Oedipus*, relating it to the drama's interplay between *tukhē* (chance) and *telos* (purpose), see Pucci's *Oedipus and the Fabrication of the Father* (a section from which is included in Bloom's collection of critical interpretations). Pucci weaves psychoanalysis with philosophy in his understanding of *Oedipus* and another critic who also takes this approach, though in a very different way, is Jonathan Lear. His essay on Sophocles' play, 'Knowingness and Abandonment: An Oedipus for Our Time' is also included in Bloom's collection. For Lear, Oedipus is 'tyrannized by what he takes to be the reasonable movement of his own mind', an unwarranted trust in the ability to know, and shuns any acknowledgement of a level of unconscious meaning in our lives, what Lear calls 'motivated irrationality'.[3]

Two of John Gould's essays have already been mentioned and one other, 'The Language of Oedipus' in his *Myth, Ritual, Memory and Exchange* is also recommended reading.

Oedipus' afterlife

The Cambridge Companion to Greek Tragedy, edited by Easterling, has two essays – 'Tragedy adapted for stages and screens: the Renaissance to the present' by Peter Burian, and 'Tragedy in performance: nineteenth- and twentieth-century productions' by Fiona Macintosh – that cover *Oedipus*. A longer study by Fiona Macintosh, *Oedipus Tyrannus*, traces Sophocles' play from its first performance in fifth-century Athens to the present day and she provides informative accounts of key productions in the theatre, as well as operas and ballets influenced by the Greek original. Henry Norman's *Account of the Harvard Greek Play*, published the year after the first modern performance of *Oedipus* in its original Greek, was republished in 2010 as part of the Cambridge Library Collection (another title in this series is a reprint of *Oedipus* that formed the first volume of Jebb's translations of Sophocles that appeared between 1883 and 1896).

Notes

1 Hall (2008), p. 166.
2 Rehm (2002), p. 1.
3 Lear (1992), p. 195, p. 201.

BIBLIOGRAPHY

Ahl, F. (1991), *Sophocles' Oedipus: Evidence & Self-Conviction*. Ithaca: Cornell University Press.

— (2008), *Two Faces of Oedipus*. Ithaca: Cornell University Press.

Aristotle (1996), *Poetics*. London: Penguin.

Armstrong, R. (1999), 'Oedipus as evidence: the theatrical background to Freud's Oedipus complex'. *PsyArt*. www.psyartjournal.com.

Arnott, P. D. (1959), *An Introduction to the Greek Theatre*. London: Macmillan.

Ballard, J. G. (2004), *Millennium People*. London: Harper Perennial.

Banville, J. (1994), *The Broken Jug*. Oldcastle: Gallery Books.

Barrett, J. (2002), *Staged Narrative: Poetics and the Messenger in Greek Tragedy*. Berkeley & London: University of California Press.

Beckett, S. (1976), *Watt*. London: John Calder.

Berkoff, S. (1994), *The Collected Plays: Volume 1*. London: Faber & Faber.

— (2000), *Plays 3*. London: Faber & Faber.

Bloom, H. (2007), *Bloom's Modern Critical Interpretations: Oedipus Rex*, Updated Edition. New York: Chelsea House.

Bradley, A. C. (1941), *Shakespearian Tragedy*. London: Macmillan.

Burgess, A. (1981), *Earthly Powers*. London: Penguin.

— (2001), *Sophocles Oedipus the King*. Minneapolis: University of Minnesota Press.

Burian, O. P. (1997), 'Myth into muthos: the shaping of tragic plots', in P. E. Easterling (ed.), *The Cambridge Companion to Greek Tragedy*. Cambridge: Cambridge University Press, pp. 178–208.

— (1997), 'Tragedy adapted for stages and screens: the Renaissance to the present', in P. E. Easterling (ed.), *The Cambridge Companion to Greek Tragedy*. Cambridge: Cambridge University Press, pp. 228–283.

— (2009), 'Inconclusive conclusion: the ending(s) of *Oedipus Tyrannus*', in S. Goldhill & E. Hall (eds), *Sophocles and the Greek Tradition*. Cambridge: Cambridge University Press, pp. 99–118.

Burian P. and Shapiro A. (eds) (2011), *The Complete Sophocles, Volume 1, The Theban Plays*. Oxford: Oxford University Press.

Bushnell, R. W. (1988), *Prophesying Tragedy*. Ithaca: Cornell University Press.

Buxton, R. (2007), 'Tragedy and Greek myth', in R. D. Woodard (ed.), *The Cambridge Companion to Greek Mythology*. Cambridge: Cambridge University Press, pp. 166–189.

Cameron, A. (1968), *The Identity of Oedipus the King*. New York: New York University Press.

Carey, J. (2009), *William Golding: The Man Who Wrote Lord of the Flies*. London: Faber & Faber.

Carlisle, T. (2000), 'Reading the scars: Rita Dove's *The Darker Face of Earth*'. *African American Review*, 34 (1), 35–150.

Carter, H. (1964), *The Theatre of Max Reinhardt*. New York: Benjamin Blom.

Clark, D. R. and McGuire J. B. (1989), *W. B. Yeats: The Writing of Sophocles' King Oedipus*. Philadelphia: American Philosophical Society.

Cocteau, J. (1967), *The Infernal Machine and Other Plays*. Translated by A. Bermal. New York: New Directions.

Corneille, P. (1980–1987), *Œuvres complètes*. Paris: Gallimard.

Dawe, R. D. (2006), *Sophocles: Oedipus Rex*. Cambridge: Cambridge University Press.

Dodds, E. R. (1968), 'On Misunderstanding the *Oedipus* Rex', in M. J. O'Brien (ed.), *Twentieth-Century Interpretations of Oedipus Rex*. Englewood Cliffs: Prentice-Hall, pp. 17–29, and in Bloom, H. (ed.), *Bloom's Modern Critical Interpretations. Oedipus Rex*, Updated Edition (2007). New York: Chelsea House, pp. 17–29.

Dove, R. (1999), *The Darker Face of the Earth*. London: Oberon Books.

Eagleton, T. (2003), *Sweet Violence: The Idea of the Tragic*. Malden, Oxford & Carlton: Blackwell Publishing.

Easterling, P. E. (1997), *The Cambridge Companion to Greek Tragedy*. Cambridge: Cambridge University Press.

Easterling, P. E. and Knox, B. M. W. (2003), *The Cambridge History of Classical Literature: Greek Drama. Vol. 1*. Cambridge: Cambridge University Press.

Edmunds, L. (2006), *Oedipus*. Abingdon & New York: Routledge.

Eidinow, E. (2011), *Luck, Fate & Fortune*. London & New York: I. B. Tauris.

Eliot, T. S. (1956), *Essays on Elizabethan Drama*. New York: Harcourt, Brace and Company.

Ewans, M. (2007), *Opera from the Greek: Studies in the Poetics of Appreciation*. Farnham: Ashgate.

Fagles, R. (1984), *Sophocles: The Three Theban Plays*. London: Penguin.

Fainlight, R. and Littman, R. J. (2009), *Sophocles: The Theban Plays*. Baltimore: The Johns Hopkins University Press.

Fergusson, F. (1949), 'Ritual and play' from *The Idea of a Theater*, in M. J. O'Brien (ed.), *Twentieth Century Interpretations of Oedipus Rex* (1968). New Jersey: Prentice-Hall, pp. 57–62.

Forster, E. M. (1992), *The Longest Journey*. London: Hodder & Stoughton.

Foster, R. (2003), *W. B. Yeats: A Life. The Arch-Poet*. Oxford: Oxford University Press.

Fóti, V. M. (2006), *Epochal Discordance: Hölderlin's Philosophy of Tragedy*. Albany: SUNY.

Freud, S. (2006), *Interpreting Dreams*. London: Penguin Books.

Fynsk, C. (1993), *Heidegger and Historicity*. Ithaca & London: Cornell University Press.

Goff, B. and Simpson, M. (2007), *Crossroads in The Black Aegean: Oedipus, Antigone and Dramas of the African Diaspora*. Oxford: Oxford University Press.

Goldhill, S. (1984), 'Exegesis: Oedipus (R)ex'. *Arethusa*, 17, 177–200.

— (1986), *Reading Greek Tragedy*. Cambridge: Cambridge University Press.

Goodhart, S. (1978), 'Ληστὰς Ἔφασκε: Oedipus and Laius' Many Murderers'. *Diacritics*, 8 (1), 55–71.

Gould, J. (2001), *Myth, Ritual, Memory, and Exchange*. Oxford: Oxford University Press.

Grab, F. D. (1972), 'Yeats' King Oedipus'. *Journal of English & Germanic Philology*, 71 (3), 336–354.

Gregory, J. (ed.) (2005), *A Companion to Greek Tragedy*. Malden, Oxford & Carlton: Blackwell Publishing.

Grene, D. and Lattimore, R. (eds) (1991), *Sophocles I: Oedipus the King, Oedipus at Colonus, Antigone*. Translated by D. Grene. Chicago. University of Chicago Press.

Hall, E. (ed.) (2008), *Oxford World Classics: Sophocles: Antigone, Oedipus the King, Electra*. Oxford: Oxford University Press.

— (2010), *Greek Tragedy: Suffering under the Sun*. Oxford: Oxford University Press.

Hall, E. and Harrop, S. (eds) (2010), *Theorising Performance*. London: Duckworth.

Harrison, G. W. M. (2000), *Seneca in Performance*. Swansea: Classical Press of Wales.

Hegel, G. F. W. (1975), *Hegel's Philosophy of Right*. Translated by T. M. Knox. Oxford: Oxford University Press.

Heidegger, M. (2000), *Introduction to Metaphysics*. New Haven & London: Yale University Press.

Herder, J. G. (1985), 'Shakespeare', in H. B. Nisbet (ed.), *German Aesthetic and Literary Criticism: Winckelmann, Lessing, Hamann,*

Herder, Schiller and Goethe. Cambridge: Cambridge University Press, pp. 161–176.

Hölderlin, F. (2001), *Hölderlin's Sophocles*. Translated by David Constantine. Tarset, Northumberland: Bloodaxe Books.

Hornblower, S. and Spawforth, A. (eds) (1998), *The Oxford Companion to Classical Civilization*. Oxford: Oxford University Press.

Hughes, T. (1969), *Seneca's Oedipus*. London: Faber & Faber.

— (1972), *Crow*. London: Faber & Faber.

Janko, R. (1999), 'Oedipus, Pericles and the plague'. *Dionysus*, 11, 15–19.

Jebb, R. C. (2004), *Sophocles: Plays Oedipus Tyrannus*. London: Bristol Classical Press.

— (2010), *Sophocles: The Plays & Fragments. Volume 1: Oedipus Tyrannus*. Cambridge: Cambridge University Press.

Jones, E. (1953), *The Life and Work of Sigmund Freud*. Vol. 1. New York: Basic Books.

Jones, J. (1980), *On Aristotle and Greek Tragedy*. London: Chatto & Windus.

Josipovici, G. (2010), *What Ever Happened to Modernism?* New Haven & London: Yale University Press.

Kant, Immanuel (2007), *Critique of Pure Reason*. Translated by Norman Kemp-Smith. Basingstoke: Palgrave.

Kierkegaard, S. (1971), *Either/Or Volume 1*. Translated by D. F. Swenson & L. M. Swenson. Princeton: Princeton University Press.

Kitto, H. D. F. (translator), Hall, E. (ed.) (2008), *Oxford World Classics: Sophocles Antigone Oedipus the King Electra*. Oxford: Oxford University Press.

Kleist, H. (1997), *Selected Writings*. Translated by David Constantine. London: Orion Publishing.

Knights, L. C. (1979), 'How many children had Lady Macbeth?', in L. C. Knights, *'Hamlet' and Other Shakespearian Essays*. Cambridge: Cambridge University Press.

Knox, B. (1957), *Oedipus at Thebes*. New Haven & London: Yale University Press.

— (1979), *Word & Action*. Baltimore and London: John Hopkins University Press.

— (1983), *The Heroic Temper: Studies in Sophoclean Tragedy*. Berkeley & London: University of California Press.

— (1984), 'Introduction', *The Three Theban Plays*. London: Penguin.

— (2007), 'Introduction to *Oedipus the King*', in H. Bloom (ed.), *Bloom's Modern Critical Interpretations: Sophocles' Oedipus Rex*, Updated edition. New York: Chelsea House Publishers, pp. 71–90.

Lattimore, R. (1967), *The Odyssey of Homer*. New York: Harper.

— (1969), *The Iliad of Homer*. Chicago: University of Chicago Press.

Lear, J. (1992), 'Knowingness and abandonment: an Oedipus for our time', in H. Bloom (ed.), *Bloom's Modern Critical Interpretations: Sophocles' Oedipus Rex*. New York: Chelsea House Publishers, pp. 183–204.

Lee Miller, P. (2007), 'Oedipus Rex revisited'. *Modern Psychoanalysis*, 31 (2), 229–250.

Lloyd-Jones, H. (1997), *Sophocles: Ajax, Electra, Oedipus Tyrannus*. Cambridge & London: Harvard University Press.

Lloyd-Jones, H. and Wilson, N. G. (eds) (1990), *Sophoclis Fabulae* (Oxford Classical Texts). Oxford: Oxford University Press.

McAuslan, I. and Affleck, J. (2003), *Sophocles Oedipus Tyrannus*. Cambridge: Cambridge University Press.

McGuinness, F. (2008), *Oedipus*. London: Faber & Faber.

Macintosh, F. (2008), 'An Oedipus for our times? Yeats's version of Sophocles' *Oedipus Tyrannos*', in M. Reverman & P. Wilson (eds), *Performance, Reception, Iconography: Studies in Honour of Olivier Taplin*. Oxford: Oxford University Press, pp. 524–547.

— (2009), *Sophocles: Oedipus Tyrannus*. Cambridge: Cambridge University Press.

Mahon, D. (2005), *Oedipus*. Oldcastle: Gallery Press.

March, J. (2009), *The Penguin Book of Classical Myths*. London: Penguin.

Milton, J. (1962), *Paradise Lost*. Edited by M. Y. Hughes. New York: Odyssey Press.

Moddelmog, D. (1993), *Readers and Mythic Signs: The Oedipus Myth in Twentieth-century Fiction*. Carbondale: Southern Illinois University Press.

Morrison, B. (1996), *The Cracked Pot*. Halifax: Northern Broadsides.

— (2003), *Oedipus/Antigone*. Halifax: Northern Broadsides.

— (2010), 'Translating Greek drama for performance', in E. Hall & S. Harrop (ed.), *Theorising Performance*. London: Duckworth, pp. 252–266.

Morrissette, B. (1960), 'Oedipus and existentialism: "Les Gommes" of Robbe-Grillet'. *Wisconsin Studies in Contemporary Literature*, 1 (3), 43–73.

Mulroy, D. (2011), *Oedipus Rex*. Madison: University of Wisconsin Press.

Murdoch, I. (1973), *The Black Prince*. London: Chatto & Windus.

Newton, R. M. (1980), 'Hippolytus and the dating of *Oedipus Tyrannus*'. *Greek, Roman and Byzantine Studies* , 21, 5–22.

Nietzsche, F. (2000), *The Birth of Tragedy*. Oxford: Oxford University Press.

Norman, H. (2010), *Account of the Harvard Greek Play*. Cambridge: Cambridge University Press.

O'Brien, M. J. (ed.) (1968), *Twentieth-Century Interpretations of Oedipus Rex*. Englewood Cliffs: Prentice-Hall.

Parker, R. (1983), *Miasma: Pollution and Purification in Early Greek Religion*. Oxford: Clarendon Press.

Pucci, P. (1992), *Oedipus and the Fabrication of the Father: Oedipus Tyrannus in Criticism and Philosophy*. Baltimore: The John Hopkins University Press.

Rabel, R. J. (2009), 'Oedipus in provence: Jean De Florette and Manon of the spring'. *Helios*, 36 (1), 67–80.

Rabinowitz, N. S. (2008), *Greek Tragedy*. Malden, Oxford & Carlton: Blackwell Publishing.

Regier, G. W. (2004), *Book of the Sphinx*. Lincoln, NE: University of Nebraska Press.

Rehm, R. (2002), *The Play of Space: Spatial Transformations in Greek Tragedy*. Princeton & Oxford: Princeton University Press.

Rotimi, O. (1974), *The Gods Are Not to Blame*. Oxford: Oxford University Press.

Rudnytsky, P. (1987), *Freud and Oedipus*. New York: Columbia University Press.

Scodel, R. (2011), *An Introduction to Greek Tragedy*. Cambridge: Cambridge University Press.

Segal, C. (1983), *Greek Tragedy*. New York: Harper & Row.

— (1993), *Oedipus Tyrannus: Tragic Heroism and the Limits of Knowledge*. Oxford: Oxford University Press.

— (1998), *Sophocles' Tragic World*. Cambridge & London: Harvard University Press.

— (1999), *Tragedy and Civilization: An Interpretation of Sophocles*. Norman: University of Oklahoma Press.

Seneca (1966), *Four Tragedies and Octavia*. Translated by E. F. Watling. London: Penguin.

Simpson, M. (2010), 'The curse of the Canon: Ola Rotimi's *The Gods Are Not to Blame*', in L. Hardwicke & C. Gillespie (eds), *Classics in Post-Colonial Worlds*. Oxford: Oxford University Press, pp. 86–101.

Sommerstein, A. (2010), *The Tangled Ways of Zeus*. Oxford: Oxford University Press.

Sophocles, Meineck, P. and Woodruff, P. (2003), *The Theban Plays*. Indianapolis: Hackett Publishing.

Stravinsky, I. (1974), *Poetics of Music in the Form of Six Lessons*. Cambridge & London: Harvard University Press.

Taplin, O. (1983), 'Emotion and meaning in Greek Tragedy', in E. Segal (ed.), *Oxford Readings in Greek Tragedy*. Oxford: Oxford University Press.

— (1986), 'Fifth-century tragedy and comedy: a synkrisis'. *The Journal of Hellenic Studies*, 106, 163–174.

— (1997), 'The pictorial record', in P. E. Easterling (ed.), *The Cambridge Companion to Greek Tragedy*. Cambridge: Cambridge University Press, pp. 69–90.

Thucydides (2009), *The Peloponnesian War*. Translated by M. Hammond. Oxford: Oxford University Press.

Turnage, M-A. (2002), *Greek*. ArtHaus Music.

Vellacott, P. (1971), *Sophocles and Oedipus*. Ann Arbor: University of Michigan Press.

Vernant, J. P. (1983), 'Ambiguity and reversal: on the enigmatic structure of *Oedipus Rex*', in E. Segal (ed.), *Oxford Readings in Greek Tragedy*. Oxford: Oxford University Press, pp. 189–209.

— (1988), 'The historical moment of tragedy in Greece: some of the social and psychological conditions', in J. P. Vernant & P. Vidal-Naquet (eds), *Myth and Tragedy in Ancient Greece* (translated by J. Lloyd). New York: Zone Books, pp. 23–28.

Vickers, S. (2008), *Where Three Roads Meet*. London: Canongate.

Voltaire (1877), *Oeuvres Completes*, Vol. II, A. Beuchot (ed.). Paris: 1877.

Walton, J. M. (2009), *Found in Translation: Greek Drama in English*. Cambridge: Cambridge University Press.

Walton, J. M. (ed.) (1998), *Sophocles Plays 1: Oedipus the King*, Oedipus at Colonus, Antigone. London: Methuen.

Watling, F. W. (1988), *Sophocles: The Theban Plays*. London: Penguin.

Wetmore, K. J. (2002), *The Athenian Sun in an African Sky: Modern African American Adaptions of Classical Greek Tragedy*. Jefferson: McFarland.

White, E. W. (1966), *Stravinsky: The Composer and His Work*. Berkeley: University of California Press.

Williams, B. (1994), *Shame and Necessity*. Berkeley: University of California Press.

Yeats, W. B. (1967), *Collected Plays of W. B. Yeats*. London. Macmillan.

Žižek, S. (1989), *The Sublime Object of Ideology*. London: Verso.

— (2002), *Did Somebody Say Totalitarianism?* London: Verso.

— (2003), *The Puppet and the Dwarf*. Cambridge, MA & London: The MIT Press.

— (2005), *Metastases of Enjoyment*. London: Verso.

INDEX